MW01680908

TAX RELIEF RESCUE

TAX RELIEF RESCUE

The Life-Saving Manual to Pull Yourself Out of IRS Debt, Put Your Feet Back on Solid Ground, and Point Yourself in the Right Direction

Kevin Roberts, MBA, EA

The Tax Relief Lifeguard™

&

Elesha Roberts,

PhD, DNP, RN, CNEcl, CNE, CHSE

TAX RELIEF RESCUE

The Life-Saving Manual to Pull Yourself Out of IRS Debt, Put Your Feet Back on Solid Ground, and Point Yourself in the Right Direction

Copyright © 2026 Kevin Roberts and Elesha Roberts
All rights reserved.

ISBN: 979-8-90343-008-6 (Paperback)
979-8-90343-009-3 (Kindle eBook)

Expert Press
www.ExpertPress.net

The information provided in this book is for informational purposes only and is not intended to be a source of advice or credit analysis with respect to the material presented. The information and/or documents contained in this book do not constitute legal or financial advice and should never be used without first consulting with an insurance and/or a financial professional to determine what may be best for your individual needs.

The publisher and the author do not make any guarantee or other promise as to any results that may be obtained from using the content of this book. You should never make any investment decision without first consulting with your own financial advisor and conducting your own research and due diligence. To the maximum extent permitted by law, the publisher and the author disclaim any and all liability in the event any information, commentary, analysis, opinions, advice, and/or recommendations contained in this book prove to be inaccurate, incomplete, or unreliable or result in any investment or other losses.

Although the author and publisher have made every effort to ensure that the information in this book was correct at press time, the author and publisher do not assume and hereby disclaim any liability to any party for any loss, damage, or disruption caused by errors or omissions, whether such errors or omissions result from negligence, accident, or any other cause.

Content contained or made available through this book is not intended to and does not constitute legal advice or investment advice, and no attorney-client relationship is formed. The publisher and the author are providing this book and its contents on an "as is" basis. Your use of the information in this book is at your own risk.

Editing by Tamma Ford
Copyediting by Lucy Spencer
Proofreading by Abby Kendall
Text design and composition by Emily Fritz
Cover design by Casey Fritz

First and foremost, to God. For sustaining me through the valleys and humbling me in the victories. Thank you for your grace, the strength to persevere, and for placing the right people in my path to guide me.

To my wife, Elesha. Years ago, I made every mistake in the book. I had the financial knowledge, but I had to hit rock bottom to gain the wisdom. It was your courage to confront me—asking, "what do you tell the people you're counseling? And you got us into this mess!"—that turned my life around. You worked three jobs to save us from my mistakes. You taught me the true meaning of dedication and showed me that knowing what to do is nothing without actually doing it. I owe it all to you.

For Hope Wooten. Your leadership went far beyond the job. Thank you for that pivotal conversation when I was eighteen, telling me I was meant for more and urging me to look beyond Beaumont. That single moment of belief gave me the courage to join the army and built the foundation for everything I have accomplished since.

For Fred Zeno. Thank you for guiding me through my transition back to civilian life and introducing me to this industry. You saw my potential before I did, and by teaching me the tax business from the ground up, you set me on a path that has defined the last twenty-five years of my life. I will never forget where I started.

And many, many others . . . Mom and Dad!

CONTENTS

PART ONE

DR. ELESHA ROBERTS

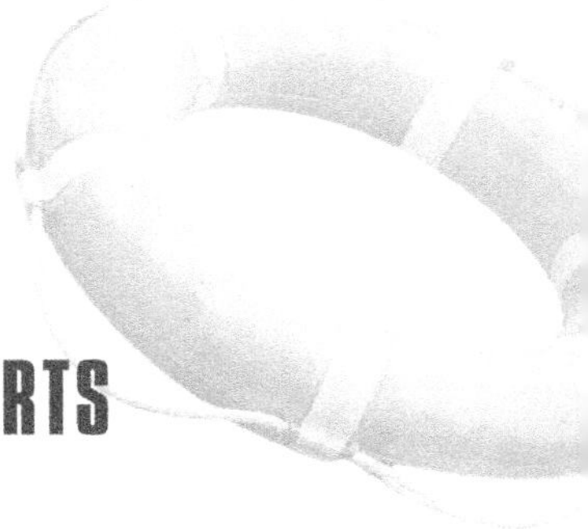

The Mental Health Side of Tax Problems and Dealing with the IRS

The exhaustion can be extreme. Physical fatigue from sleepless nights that are far too short. Weariness from working long hours or multiple jobs just to keep up. Emotional depletion from having no social life or downtime. Mental torture from constant worrying about how long you can keep up the pace.

When you're in that state of emotional, physical, and mental strain, you can't help but trigger arguments, flare up at people trying to help you, and beat yourself up over every single bad money decision you ever made.

Fear and anxiety really take a toll on your mental and physical health and your relationships. When you're going through the motions for appearances' sake on the outside while you're emotionally drained and emotionally tired on the inside, that's not living.

If you take no action, the spiral of exhaustion will take you down. It will intensify *until you address the cause and deal with it.* That is what our book will help you do.

CHAPTER 1

GARNISHMENT!

When I first got the news that my paycheck was going to be garnished, and then saw by how much, it was a very frightening and painful moment.

At that time, Kevin and I had been married about six years, after dating for five. Though we were not newlyweds, we were still in a new relationship and life management space. We were still seeing what was going on in the marriage and learning to connect with each other.

I had my finances; he had his finances. We always knew what was going on a little bit with each other's money, but I never really paid attention that deeply. I just knew when I went to my full-time job as a registered nurse, I'd get a check for X amount. I was working to make a living, to take care of our household. I wasn't involved in Kevin's business operations. My career was on this side; his business was on that side.

When I got that notice at work that Payroll was going to be taking "a certain amount" out of my check per IRS order, it took me off guard. I had an instant, emotional reaction. I was in disbelief at first. "Oh, there must be some mistake." Then, I panicked. "What obligation did I forget? What have I done wrong?" Finally, it hit that this was not some vague, passing event. It was . . . the IRS?! That stirred up anxiety. "Why did the *IRS* want my paycheck?! *What* is going on here?"

I ran to Kevin because he is our financial planning guy in the marriage. He was in charge of doing all our finances at that time. I brought the notice home from work. I looked him in the eye, "Hey, what is this? Do I need to go and talk to someone in HR, Payroll, or what? What *is* this?"

I just didn't know what to do with that. I'd never gotten anything like that notice before.

You guessed it: My paycheck was being *garnished*.

That was when Kevin had to face the facts. He had to come clean about what had happened in his business to bring the garnishment on. Kevin had defaulted on an SBA loan.

The US Department of the Treasury was the collection agency in this case. Who knew? Not me! Well, the US Department of the Treasury (legally, I might add) turned to my full-time nursing paycheck, which was the most stable at that time.

Kevin had launched his business by taking out personal loans and using credit cards—his and mine. Later, when that money wasn't enough, the SBA loan helped keep the business afloat.

I frankly didn't know the extent of the financial overreach until that garnishment came along. I did not have the full picture at the beginning. I didn't have all the facts for some time because this whole incident was just a gift that kept on giving.

Neither of us had a lot of mentorship role models growing up. We had no one who taught us, no one to talk to about finances and money management. We definitely did not know how to be an entrepreneur or start a business. It was here that some of that mentorship, some education, would have been helpful. Who do you go to when the US government is knocking down your door? Who do you know with the knowledge and experience to truly help? My goodness! I didn't even know the right questions to ask for clarity or support.

One of the things that really drew me to my husband is that he was always very financially savvy and a big dreamer. Now more than ever, he is more knowledgeable than most people, and believe it or not, that was true even during this time. He knows numbers, he speaks the language (financial language). I always felt very comfortable talking with him about money matters and having him lead that part of our marriage relationship. But other than the two of us, we had no financial mentors to emulate.

The financial pressure was on both of us from the day that garnishment hit. I was counting on my usual 100 percent paycheck and came home with only 15 percent of it. You read that correctly. I was left with fifteen cents on the dollar. That's the scary part. Pressures built because we had to pay bills, eat, and survive on 15 percent—with no end in sight. That day, I believed I'd be getting 15 percent . . . indefinitely. That wasn't true, but I didn't know that yet. So? I was not calm, cool, or collected with Kevin. Not one bit.

I thought about my "nonnegotiables" and discussed them with Kevin. At that time, we had had a mortgage for only a year or so. Payments could not be missed. We had our first son, who was a toddler in a paid day care. Payments for that could not be missed, either. We were committed to paying anything needed for our child. Kevin's car was paid off, but I had a new car with payments. That was one of the first brand-new things that I had bought myself, and it was a big-ticket item that came with a loan. I wasn't about to let that go. We didn't see the light at the end of this tunnel for a long time.

Kevin's words to me throughout this journey would always be "We're okay. We're okay."

Sleepless Nights and Bad Decisions

In a time like this, you have some sleepless nights. You wake up trying to figure it out in your brain. When you're in that state of emotional, physical, and mental strain and tiredness, you can't help but trigger an argument with your spouse. You get upset even with other people who are trying to help you. You're exhausted. No good decision was ever made from worry and tiredness.

Oh, my middle-of-the-night worries were painful! I would wake up thinking about everything that needed to be paid that week, and every month. The financial pressure would start at the beginning of the month and build and build. We'd make it to the end of the month with some relief. Then the financial pressure would start all over again the following month. For years.

In my case, the exhaustion was triple: I wasn't sleeping enough, which drained me physically. I worked long hours and held down three jobs instead of one. I had no social life or free time anymore. That was emotionally draining. I worried, which is a mental nightmare all day long. Every time I had downtime, I worried in my head and my heart, "Can I keep this up?" I worried during every spare moment, and that was mentally exhausting.

Action, Action, Action

I would say that the thing that helped me throughout that whole period was action. You get out of hopelessness by taking action. Just one step in the right direction is comforting.

We took three main actions right away.

1. Kevin got accepted into a US Department of the Treasury repayment program for his SBA loan.

2. My immediate action was to secure more income that paid well. I had the skills for that to happen. I was already working full-time as an RN, a registered nurse. I was a university faculty member teaching nursing students. I also picked up an adjunct, weekend position. I couldn't even tell you how many hours I worked. I felt like I worked more than I slept. I look back and realize that I did!

3. Together, we were writing up a cash-only spending budget. We worked on it repeatedly over two or three months. It was writing out how much we spent and detailing what we spent it on. We had never kept track of every penny of spending before like this. Not once. Not in this kind of detail. Not even Kevin, who is the ultra-frugal one in the family.

Triggers

I teach psychiatric nursing. We often talk about *triggers.* Basically, a trigger (in the mental health field) is something happening now that reminds a person of a bad experience from their past. It can make them feel that old negative emotion again (fear, anger, etc.), even if they are in reality totally safe. A trigger can be anything—a sound, something someone says, or an event. Triggers make it hard to stay calm.

Worry is a version of fear. Anxiety is a stronger version of fear, and panic is the strongest version of fear. Any of those feelings can be triggered. It seems like it's out of the blue, but something always underlies the immediate surge of that feeling.

Well, let me admit now that I discovered some of my own triggers during this crisis! I started noticing things that triggered me emotionally. They sent me down a negative or downward kind of spiral. A bill collector sends a notice? Triggered. A random spam call that I wouldn't even answer? Triggered. Some random company knew my name, or got my email or phone number? Triggered. I would instantly wonder, "What do they *want from me?!* Who *are* they?" It might not even have been in relation to our debt (because we do receive a *lot* of spam calls), but it would trigger me to feel a certain awful way. The worst case of these triggers was when it would set off an argument with Kevin instead of a calm-headed conversation with him. Emotions were riding high back then. It was really rough during that time.

The "What's coming *next*?" was also triggering for me. I didn't really know what to expect. I found myself waiting for the other shoe to drop, so to speak.

Married people reading this might wonder how I could not know what was happening. Well, the US Department of the Treasury doesn't just email you. They don't call you up. They snail-mail you. Given our schedules and routines, it was Kevin who would check the mailbox at home. He had never mentioned any letters he got at work. That's why I don't remember the SBA part of the warnings. The garnishment was my first clue.

Cutting Back

Kevin has always been a real stickler on money and finances. I mean, even when we dated, he was that way. We dated for five years before we got married, and he was always financially savvy. That was one of the things I did and still do love about him. That's one of the reasons why I felt comfortable with him taking the lead in a lot of our financial affairs after we got married.

Be warned: Debt can happen to the best-intended people.

Kevin has always been frugal, but when my garnishment hit, we went beyond that. We became very, very minimalist. When I say minimalist, it was, in fact, survival mode. We didn't go out to eat anymore, not at all. We purchased nothing new. We ate very modestly—cheap and affordable meals that we could make at home (beans and rice). We attacked debt in the Dave Ramsey snowballing way (more on that later). We always crunched those numbers for how we could make sure that my checks from my three jobs covered us for everything our family needed. The keyword was *need*. We stopped doing that American "instant gratification" type of spending.

It was after two-plus years of working those three jobs that I really started seeing changes in our income. It took about that long for our budgeting and debt payment approach to start shining a light at the end of the tunnel for me.

Now, Kevin will tell you the details, but I had only that one check garnished. I got 15 percent of my usual paycheck amount, just that one time. I'd feared, though, that it would be endless. It was not. Kevin did take action with the IRS, as he will explain. But if he had not taken the *right* action *right away*, the IRS would have continued to draw from my next paychecks too. If he had not done what was needed right then, we would have continued with my 15 percent for the duration of the mess we were in.

Kevin did take action. He assured me that my other paychecks were safe. They were smaller. That garnished check was from my most consistent, full-time, full-benefits, highest-paying job.

As we both write this part of the story, it brings back memories of deep hurt. That lived experience is why we are writing this book for you, even though it has taken us many years to get to it.

Let me say again that taking action right away was crucial. Back then, we did take action once the garnishment hit. It took that jolt for Kevin to end his avoidance of the issue.

Because we took action, the situation did not break us. It did not break our ability to pay for our life. It did not break our marriage relationship. We did not lose the house or my car. Our son got the things he needed. Kevin did not lose his business. *Because we took action.*

I say, if it doesn't break you, it does make you stronger. People say it, and it's so cliché, but it is so true. Our bond strengthened. There is nothing that can come between us now.

Silence Is Not Golden!

Before the cool-headed conversations could flow again, I admit to you that we both experienced a version of burnout. We just had no words. We were not talking. Those daily discussions weren't happening at first. There were days that we were both in a space of, "I don't have anything else to say. We've already fought. And guess what? I'm exhausted from fighting."

In my head, my words were, "I don't want to fight anymore. I don't want to talk about the phone calls coming to me. I don't want to talk about the letters. I don't want to talk about our financial plan. I don't want to have anything positive to even say to you, Mr. Roberts. Not even good morning. I don't want to say that because I'm mad at you and I'm just tired."

Silence ruled the house too often at the beginning.

We wanted to give up many times. The whole thing was so exhausting on every level. There were times that we wanted to give up, but we leaned on God, so we didn't give up.

Today, it can be funny at home if Kevin gets quiet. He's always been a naturally calm, soft-spoken, quiet man.

Today, our two kids are older, and they know about this situation and how it influences our lives. They can also tell when something is going on. The older one will say, "Mom, I don't like it when Dad gets quiet. If I've done something wrong, I'd rather have Dad scold me, correct me, and give me my punishment. But Mom, when Dad gets quiet, I know I'm really in trouble."

I have to say that, from the outside, it looked like we were still functioning and still doing what needed to be done. That's what a lot of people do. They go through the motions for appearances' sake. But they're emotionally drained and emotionally tired inside. When they stop fighting is when they stop talking. When they stop interacting with family, with friends, that's a real warning sign.

Keep those lines of communication open, even if it's emotional. Even if it's embarrassing to say the words you have to say.

Communication Back on Track

Now, if you are going through this kind of debt, you have to involve your partner. As I stated, the garnishment was my first clue. It was my partner, my spouse, who knew of the problem. I did not. If you don't involve your partner, he or she might be in for an unwelcome shock. I was.

That person could be your business partner. That partner could be your spouse. If you have children, consider how it can affect your kids. If you are close with other family, it can worry them to watch how you are handling things or how you are falling apart. A lot of people will probably be affected by your debt, whether you acknowledge it or not.

Kevin didn't have a business partner. He had me. Our son was really young, just a toddler. It wasn't anything he felt or understood, of course. Older kids sense what's going on, but he was too young. I was the one. I was emotional, fearful, and angry because I did not want my kid to be affected by this overwhelming amount of debt. I went into Mama Bear mode, you could say. Our child would only know safety. End of story.

I feel it's one thing to argue about an issue. We're going to yell it out. We're going to fight it out. Then we calm down a bit, and we're going to talk about a plan. But it's another thing to not talk at all.

Total silence should not be a tool for managing problems in a partnership. You cannot solve a shared problem if you refuse to discuss it. A hard, hard thing we did that helped us was that we started *talking* more about money issues and our finances in general. We had to. Silence on this subject would have broken us.

You're married. You have a business partner. You need to discuss ordinary life issues, ordinary business concerns. You need to face the elephant in the room.

We had a new financial plan we could both agree to, because we talked about what it should be. We were taking action and talking about what those actions should be, too.

If something new did come up around money, we would address it together and right away. We wouldn't let it linger.

But in the beginning, communication was really difficult. We broke down that wall of silence and started talking about it (well, I do admit to yelling and shouting a lot at first).

We talked through the fears. We talked through our worries and our anxiety. I found that having those talks, having a plan, reduced my fears. This said, I can't deny that in those couple of years, being overwhelmed with fear was my biggest emotional hit. However, we are religious people; we do believe in God and depend on God. I can't say we ever broke to the point where there was no return. We weren't yelling at God; we were counting on God—100 percent.

Kevin was right there with me on this, and having someone else depending on us helped us to be that much more resilient. It helped us keep talking about this and everything else. It might have been different if it had been just the two of us. I think that if it had just been him and me, we still would have made it, of course. I think the fact that we had our son and he was so young got us more focused on changing what we both came from.

As for me, due to that garnishment and Kevin's debts, I got a financial wake-up call. Up until that point, I had accepted my parents' ways of managing money. I knew that had to change. This debt was my big wake-up call that I knew nothing valid about money management! It was

Kevin's and my shared wake-up call that we had to organize our financial life differently.

Adapting Is Key

In a real way, I have tried to block that whole period of our lives out of my memory because things are good now. In the heat of that moment, though, I tried very hard to adapt. I know that because of my husband's prior military experience (and just by how he's wired to think), he has always talked about adapting and overcoming. This was just one of those things you dealt with in the moment. You did everything that you could to get through it and survive. And then once you're over it, you don't want to go back and relive it.

Now we're in a great position, very well taken care of. We've definitely come out on the other side of this, but now and then, I still feel a little bit of angst because those triggers I mentioned are still active. Hiding, but still there. Today, we both have better coping mechanisms. We always immediately talk to each other.

Living the Lessons

Along with the lessons that it's always preferable to talk through the problems and to keep a solutions-focused approach, there were the money-management lessons. That won't surprise any of you.

Like so many others, we had been using credit cards. That stopped hard and suddenly with our new financial management plan. We learned to spend only cash. We budgeted tightly, and for the first time, for a cash-only, needs-only lifestyle.

That meant we had to spend with attention. No more instant-gratification purchases. No more swiping that credit card without thinking much about it. In our credit card culture, we'll swipe that card so quickly. That was why it took us some months to get clear on our actual spending. Our only "card" usage now is the debit card for gas and big purchases. We are always in such a hurry that we want to just stand right there at the gas pump with the debit card to fill it up and go. But we use only our debit cards, never any credit cards. As everyone knows, the debit card only works if you have money in that account, so it "acts like" cash. Right now, I can tell you what we spend on groceries (and most of our bills) to the dollar every month. That's because, all these years later, we still run a cash-only household. Lesson learned.

CHAPTER 2

THE PSYCHOLOGY OF IRS FEAR

Fear is real. When fear is intentionally instilled in you, it can be paralyzing, or it can be motivating.

When anyone—Kevin's clients, you, your friends, your family—gets a letter from the IRS, it is scary.

I must say that all of those letters are doing *exactly* what they are designed to do. Don't just believe me. Read what an actual former commissioner of the IRS Small Business/Self-Employed Division, Darren Guillot, said at the American Society of Tax Problem Solvers (ASTPS) Super Conference of 2024 (bolding is mine):

> *"The majority of the IRS's revenue is collected through taxpayers who voluntarily file their returns and make payments, typically followed by the distribution of relevant notices.* ***Behavioral psychologists and doctoral***

> ***experts developed these notices, ensuring their effectiveness was intentional.*** *They strategically design notices using behavioral science, deciding where to highlight, underline, place words, QR codes, and phone numbers to guide recipients' responses. The IRS has used these methods since at least 2017, with ongoing support from the current commissioner. In 2024, thirty-one more notices were redesigned; the IRS collection was first to introduce QR codes on notices in 2020. This change led to fewer calls and improved access to irs.gov, while also making it easier for voice bots to assist callers—a notable success."*

Another presentation made in 2023 at the ASTPS Super Conference discussed aspects of how the letters are drafted *according to human behavioral science.*[1] These are not AI- or bot-generated letters. They are human-crafted to create a response from you. That fact is out there and public.

Why IRS Letters Feel Overwhelming

Let me break it down.

- Every IRS letter is intentionally designed to scare you. They are actually written to stir up anxiety and fear in you.

1 The ASTPS Super Conference is a recognized annual industry event where IRS leadership and other experts convene. https://www.astps.org/; https://www.astps.org/super-conference-schedule-download/. Accessed December 2025.

- Every IRS letter is intentionally designed to motivate you to take action. The psychologists the IRS employs to write them know all about fear as a motivator.

- Every letter is intentionally designed to fix your broken system. Your money-management system is broken. Your system for taking care of your financial and tax obligations is broken. The IRS can't collect from your broken system. It is scaring you into fixing it. It wants the money you owe them, and it is frightening you (a.k.a. motivating you) into paying it!

- Every *successive* IRS communication with you is intentionally designed to reignite the fear that will finally motivate you to fix things.

So each successive letter you get until you take action is doing exactly what it is designed to do. It puts that fear into you and says, "Hey, wake up. Something is going on that needs fixing, that needs your immediate attention." The IRS, through its letters, is doing exactly what it intended to do: It is getting you to really wake up and take action.

The IRS wants to get what is owed to the government. Of course they do. Whether it is Kevin's SBA loan repayment or your tax debts, we tend to forget that the IRS is just one big, enormous collection agency.

Those psychologists who draft the letters sitting unopened on top of your fridge know how human emotions and the human mind work. They understand *and use* human psychology as leverage over you.

If those IRS letters said things in a nice way, we wouldn't be responsive. I know I wouldn't be. You wouldn't be motivated to get in touch with the IRS or a professional. You wouldn't do what needed to be done to solve the problem.

Since our debt issue all those years ago, Kevin has turned it around to help others in similar cases. He is now fully trained by the IRS. How's that for turning things upside down? He's an IRS Enrolled Agent (EA)[2] and helps individuals and businesses with tax debt. He knows the tax code inside-out (please, let me brag a minute) so that he can get the right resolution for his clients. But back then? He was a struggling entrepreneur with a money-losing business.

I will say that Kevin understands debt to the government better than some other people in the industry. I think this is because of his lived experience, first of all. Also, because of his EA training, he knows what the IRS is trying to get from you and what needs to be done. He comes at it with a different context from other EAs. I believe that. He makes it more like a humanizing process to say, "Hey, they are wagging their fingers at you. They're basically looking at you and telling you to do this one thing right now." He

2 "Enrolled agent information," https://www.irs.gov/tax-professionals/enrolled-agents/enrolled-agent-information. Accessed December 2025.

talks you through your obligations, responsibilities, and the action you need to take right now. He can reassure you because he understands what the IRS is looking for. Kevin will help you to give the authorities what they need. That way, both the IRS and you are taken care of.

I love the fact that Kevin has lived that dual experience. First, he was the indebted man dealing with the IRS for himself, on his own. Now he's the resolutions man, dealing with the IRS on your behalf from sound training and education. Let him translate. Let him interpret for you. Let him plan with you. Working with him will dramatically reduce your fear.

When you need to make sense of what your risks and solutions are, Kevin's the expert now.

That emotional toll when you get the letter stating they've garnished your paycheck is real. The emotional toll and embarrassment are real when they seize your assets. It is scary. The IRS *intends for it to be scary.* That's when you need to have someone that you trust who has experience speaking the IRS's language.

Frankly, I could have never, ever dealt with the IRS on my own back then. It's just like any specific field. I'm a nurse; in nursing, we have our own language, our own abbreviations, our shorthand. In the military, it's the same way. I don't understand any of their abbreviations or any of their acronyms. The IRS also has its own language, and you want an individual who speaks that language to represent and help you.

Fight, Flight, Freeze: The Psychology of Avoidance

It was Kevin's debt. He got the IRS letters at his office and at home. I found out on the very day of my garnishment that he had hidden the letters and the whole scope of the debt from me. He hid them, just like some of his clients ignore them. He tells me how his new clients will bring him unopened letters from the IRS that they received months earlier.

It's fear. It's a protective mechanism. Fear is your mind protecting you from an unknown, from a scary all-powerful government agency. That expression "it's all in your mind" is true. Fear is mental, first and foremost.

But remember this aspect of fear that I mentioned earlier:

When fear is intentionally instilled in you, it can be paralyzing . . . or it can be motivating.

The Mind Game

This is where the psychology part comes in. Fear is a mind game, and the IRS plays it like a master.

People convince themselves, "If I don't see that letter and I don't open it, then I don't have to deal with it—not with the letter, but also not with the debt. If I don't read it, it doesn't exist."

I think Kevin really did get very good at that denial and avoidance back then. That's our human protective mechanism inside our brain that says, "If I don't see it, I don't have to deal with it today." And that's to our detriment, because it's going to keep coming. It's going to be that gift that keeps on giving until you deal with it.

This is the best strategy I can give you:

Get ahead of the debt by taking action.

That's why they say that hindsight is 20/20. A lot of people go into denial; that's our way of coping with it. Remember:

Fear is a mind game, and the IRS plays it like a master.

The Stress Spiral of Financial Pressure

Now, let me be the trained mental health professional for a moment. Let me use my nursing language to tell you about the "stress spiral" phenomenon.

In a stress spiral, an initial stressor (that IRS collections letter, that garnishment notification) activates strong emotional reactions. Like me, you could experience anxiety and worry because you're facing the unknown. You could, like me, experience irritability, because I growled, "How could my husband get us into such a mess?!" You could go through some sadness because the resolution takes years, and you don't see a light at the end of the tunnel right now.

Your thoughts are racing; your mind is rehashing disaster scenarios over and over.

Those negative emotional hits to your well-being then lead to secondary problems—you can't sleep, you withdraw from those who normally support you, or you're not as able to do a job as usual. All those things become *new* stressors and further intensify the original distress. It spirals.

There you go. That's my nurse's definition of what Kevin and I were going through.

The stress spiral is set in motion by the unknown. In our case, it started when we didn't have a detailed, regular tracking handle on our finances, and our income took a hit. We didn't pay attention to our very real obligations around that money. You must get a good handle on your responsibilities. And if you don't, or you don't know how? Stress builds.

Now, for Kevin to take action, he needed a major trigger (the garnishment and my sudden involvement in an issue he'd kept from me). Most people do. Fear is a motivator, but in cases like this, just that first scary letter from the IRS isn't enough.

Let me repeat this:

Just that first scary letter from the IRS is probably not enough. Every successive letter is also designed to further scare you into action.

The risks escalate. The pressure is stronger with each letter.

Our trigger to take action was the garnishment. It is a late trigger (as Kevin will show you) and comes just before a levy (and he'll explain that to you too).

In our adult brains, we get warnings all the time about our obligations and responsibilities in life. "Hey, I'm not filing my taxes on time this year if I don't get going right now. Did I take out the right deductions? Did I claim the right number of dependents for my withholdings with my payroll department? Do I have all my backup receipts?"

We know that these obligations and responsibilities exist. Nonetheless, we also sometimes think, "But no worries. I'm the little guy. The IRS, the government, they're not looking for *me*. They're after the rich people. They're after big, cheating corporations. They're not going to catch up with *me* anytime soon."

I don't want to say that people are intentionally trying to defraud the government, but I think that we know it when we haven't taken care of business or fulfilled the obligations we have. We do know we have those obligations. Taxes and laws? They're a hard pill. However, as the saying goes, ignorance of the law is no excuse for breaking it.

At the time of my garnishment, I knew I was doing everything right. I was showing up to work. I had my taxes taken out through withholding. I married the tax guy! I "knew" he was taking care of our taxes. He was doing my dad's taxes. I knew he had the information and the skill. I didn't know cash flow was so bad in his business that the credit card debt was a mountain, and the business taxes he owed weren't paid. I didn't know he wasn't covering his business's obligations on the SBA loan. I didn't know any of his business problems until that first day or two after the garnishment.

On his side, Kevin was in denial that his business debt issue might overflow into our household. It wasn't just a business matter anymore. When he saw the consequences on our household, that moved him to take action.

Fear as a Motivator

The IRS *counts on* that fear. That fear the IRS creates when they send you a letter or garnish your paycheck is real and 100 percent intended. When it is your spouse's paycheck, because you don't have anything to garnish on your side (our case), there will be fear, but there will also be anger and blame. There is definitely a psychology to it, and have no doubt—the IRS letter writers know it!

When we think about how the government is structured, we might not know every aspect of the government and why it does certain things the way that it does, and why we need to do certain things the way that we do them. There is definitely a process. There are definitely rules that need to be followed. When I think about the psychology aspect of it, you really need to do a deep dive into what you believe and what is required of you from the IRS.

Remember that one characteristic of fear is that it can *motivate* you to take action and do what needs to be done to be successful. If you are finally motivated to take action, you should talk to someone who knows how the IRS thinks, who knows the tax code, and speaks the language of the IRS and its agents. I promise you, Kevin is that professional. He is trained and, therefore, very knowledgeable about the tax code and the IRS way of thinking. He knows tax resolution processes and procedures.

We both know firsthand the fear and the stress on a marriage, on a household, on a relationship that a scary debt can create. He addresses that in his talks with clients.

Hard-Headed Humans

Fear is a motivator, and the IRS knows it. It also knows that one letter—that first letter they send to a delinquent taxpayer—won't create such a *sustained* fear that you are moved to action. That's why they line up those letters and keep them coming: to motivate you to take action. If you take no action? They just scare you again with another letter that escalates your risks. And again and again. We are a hard-headed species! That's what happened to Kevin, because garnishment is not the first thing but the last resort of the IRS to get you to pay what you owe.

We don't, as American taxpayers, know the extent of the IRS's powers and tactics. We usually fear what we don't know. So we tremble. We don't take action. But when we don't act, it eats at us. We have this underlying anxiety all the time. Fear and anxiety are joined in that stress spiral.

In my profession, we talk about levels of anxiety. The milder or moderate anxiety level is motivating because that's what tells you, "Hey, take action to fix this." Levels of anxiety escalate if you stay in it too long. Don't let it turn into a high-level, paralyzing panic attack.

Address the cause. Deal with it. Be done with the stress. Let this fear and anxiety do its *positive* job, which is to motivate you to do better and take action. If you take no action, the anxiety will eat away at your well-being. Fear and anxiety really take a toll on your mental health, on your overall health, on your family's well-being.

I'm biased, I know, but I have to say that Kevin's mild manner should soothe anyone's anxiety. He's so calm. His voice is so quiet. I'll be yelling and flailing my arms around, "Kevin, the house is on fire!!!" and he'll just quietly say, "We're okay, we're going to be all right. Everybody just follow me out of the house now, okay?" The house was figuratively on fire when my paycheck was garnished. I screamed and shouted and jumped up and down. Yes. I did that. Kevin, though? He was quietly on the phone with the IRS, so that the one garnishment was all I had. He was, finally, motivated to take action. If you are procrastinating, believe me when I say, he understands why!

As his spouse, I had to be involved in the solution, or he would never have succeeded. Remember that, if you are in a marriage or a business partnership. You have to involve your partner. You have to communicate the reality to your partner. Silence is not golden. Not when the IRS is writing to you. Not when you have partners and family involved.

What we don't know is what kills us. I certainly see that from my nursing and health care perspective. If you or someone you know has a federal (IRS) tax debt or any federal debt for which the IRS is the collection agency, Kevin is who you want to go to.

PART TWO

KEVIN ROBERTS

The Tax Side and Resolution of Your Debt

As Elesha has described, ignoring your tax obligations is a risk to your peace of mind and your marriage, not to mention your financial security. As the one who brought this problem to our family, I can attest that every word she writes is the truth.

Ignoring your tax obligations will negatively affect more than just your business partnership. For businesses, a tax debt at the company level has a trickle-down effect that you want to avoid. Failure to address tax debt can ruin your business reputation, its ability to continue earning, and even worse.

The IRS can take actions against the individual taxpayer that are embarrassing and confusing. It can take actions against a business that cause you to lose clients, vendors, and employees.

Don't wave any red flags at the IRS! Don't ignore their letters. When you're falling far behind in your ability to resolve your debt, the cost of not taking action increases.

The bottom line on both the personal and business fronts is that it's just not worth it. Know your obligations. Assume your responsibilities. I can help you with that.

CHAPTER 3

BEST LAID PLANS

I joined the army right after graduation. Years later, after I was married, I opened a tax preparation franchise.

In that franchise, I was a financial counselor, but I knew nothing about running a business. I made every mistake in the book. My revenue looked great on paper. But that spreadsheet didn't mean I had any money to take home. Things got so tight that I started using credit in my wife's name (yes, yes, I know) just to keep things afloat. I had hit rock bottom—and here is the story of what "rock bottom" meant in my case.

Shoestring Launch

I opened a tax prep franchise even though I was unable to get the financing that I needed. During the first couple of years, I was just paying all the bills with my credit cards. Yes, I launched my business with a heavy use of credit cards. I struggled to even pay those monthly minimums. It was a near thing for many months. I took out a personal loan to keep going.

After those couple of hard years, I qualified for and received an SBA loan, and money issues evened out. From that point, everything was going great. Two more years went by. I found that I wasn't able to make those payments on the SBA loan, so I stopped. I just stopped making those loan reimbursement payments.

About a year later, I got the first of several nasty letters from the bank saying I needed to pay my loan.

Now I know this is a book about taxes and tax debt. I hear some of you asking, "Kevin, tell us about taxes, not about loans."

Here's a thing many people fail to realize (and Elesha spilled the beans to you). Small Business Administration (SBA) loans are federally guaranteed loans. Yes, our local banks manage them and seem to be the ones approving them. But you're on a federal government program with an SBA loan. That means the US Department of the Treasury is the actual creditor. When you stop paying the US Department of the Treasury what you owe, the IRS gets involved.

Why is that? The US Department of the Treasury is not a collection agency. The Internal Revenue Service (IRS) is. But I'll get to that in a minute.

When those letters from my lending bank started to arrive, I ignored them. Oh, I opened them. I read them. I got scared. I was really nervous. But I took no action.

Then the feds took our income tax refund check. Here we were, expecting that refund check. Nothing. Elesha's and my expected thousands in refunds went right back to the IRS. Even though the IRS took our whole income tax refund check that year, the amount didn't pay down the full past-due SBA amount. It paid down only a small portion of it.

Even after they took the refund check, my wife, Elesha, was still not aware of this whole story. She had little to no information. She didn't know I had defaulted on the SBA loan. As she stated, we knew a little about each other's work and business matters, but just high level. I was running the business, and she wasn't involved in any part of it. She didn't know such details. That changed when she started receiving phone calls saying that a certain household bill was not paid. Those were "past-due" calls, this time for household bills.

I kept denying problems, saying that I was making payments. Not the best strategy, granted.

Well, a very few months later, Elesha's paycheck was garnished. She got 15 (yes, *only* 15) percent of her usual check amount. That was a shocker to her; there's no denying it. When she came home that evening, all anxious and confused, so was I. The garnishment was news to me because I was not the one notified. The US Department of the Treasury wrote to her employer about the coming garnishment. Her payroll or human resources department let her know by letter that they would be garnishing a certain portion of a check. Then, a week later, she saw the actual amount left in her check.

That very night, in our usually peaceful home, all hell broke loose.

It was more than an oops-oh-boy, because from that point on, our relationship was really shaky.

She was panicking. She was saying (well, sometimes yelling), "How did you get into such *debt*? How could you let it *go* this far?" and so on.

Now I knew I had to take action. No more sitting on my hands. No more avoiding the elephant in the room. This was crunch time. We no longer had enough to pay the bills for our household. First, because I wasn't bringing any money home from my business. There was no money from the business. It was that bad. Also, if all we had was 15 percent of Elesha's full-time pay moving forward, we couldn't pay even the smallest bills for our household.

Well, while I was figuring that out, Elesha's first step was separating our financial and bank accounts. She didn't mention that to you, but she was a whirlwind. She closed joint accounts. She opened single-owner accounts. She was scared. She was right.

It took me nearly two weeks to even find the right agency to contact. I didn't know back then what I know today about IRS operations, procedures, and such. At the time, I was just a tax preparer, a financial counselor. Once I found out who to talk to and what to do and I committed to doing it, the garnishment was suspended. Elesha only had the one paycheck garnished. The IRS paused the garnishment. Just having been in touch with the right agency, committing to taking action, and signing an agreement about it with the IRS, I got us some breathing room.

The SBA loans are largely (but not 100 percent) federally guaranteed.[3] I hadn't disappeared to some non-extradition country. I wasn't sending money to illegal offshore accounts. Because of those two factors, I was able to negotiate an *"offer in compromise"* for myself (more on that later). It was clear to the IRS (finally) that my business was failing and I had no cash flow to pay the loan and all other bills, too. Making that case reduced my amount owed quite a lot. But I still owed a sum of money to the IRS for the SBA loan *on top of* my credit card debts. *On top of* what I had spent on Elesha's credit cards. *On top of* that non-SBA personal loan I had also taken out.

---

3 SBA loan basics: https://www.sba.gov/partners/lenders/7a-loan-program/terms-conditions-eligibility#percentage-of-guaranty. Accessed December 2025.

Collection Agency

The government interconnection is that the US Department of the Treasury uses the IRS to collect debt. The IRS is one great big collection agency for taxes, but also for collections on behalf of other federal agencies.[4] This is why this particular story of ours is so relatable to the topic we're discussing in this book.

I had to get all of my business financials together. I was required to provide a detailed collection of data about the business with supporting documents. It included how much the business was making or losing, of course, but even more than that. The offer in compromise went through in about three months.

The SBA loan works differently from a traditional bank loan due to its federal sourcing and guarantees. Because of my default, even all these years later, I could never get any type of federal assistance.

I had to figure out, financially, how to honor the IRS agreement. From a financial business perspective of what happened, things were still hard. While this franchise was designed to do business year-round, tax preparation really only makes money between February and June. After June or July, it is very unpredictable when you only do tax preparation. The business didn't have enough money coming in

4 Student loans are in this category when they are funded by taxpayer dollars via the Department of Education. The government guarantees at least partial repayment, covers defaults to a degree, and offers relief like income-driven plans and forgiveness programs. Such defaults are collected by the IRS through the Federal Offset Program (TOP).

during the off-season. Today, I know it was because I didn't run the numbers. I didn't know I should raise the prices on my services or by how much. I kept the business going for another two years after Elesha's garnishment. Then I called it. I closed it down.

The takeaways for me from this period of my life and those experiences are something I can share with you. Those experiences inspired my current career as a tax-debt resolution professional. Our experiences have driven how I serve clients today. I was drowning in debt, including to the government. I had put my family and our personal financial well-being at risk. I had to learn. Now I share these lessons with every client.

Lessons Learned

1. Be proactive. You can do that by knowing the rules. Know your numbers. Know best practices. Keeping accurate, separate, written personal and business records is the best way to know how your business is doing—and notably, whether it is making or losing money. Recordkeeping is proactive. My biggest issue back then was procrastination, but another one was poor recordkeeping. I didn't bother to learn how to keep timely, accurate records. I learned. You must do the same.

Any time the government is involved—and it almost always is—you need to be proactive about all your money management. "Relentless" describes the IRS when you owe them money. Prevention means you are also relentless in tracking your money in real time and knowing and respecting your obligations and responsibilities.

2. Don't get into debt. Don't launch or operate your business or your household through debt. Yes, it might be required at some points of the business's life (growing the business is one). But don't run daily operational expenses or payroll (anything!) through debt.

3. Charge enough for your services so that you can pay all the bills and still bring home a great income for your household. Otherwise, why be in business at all? Keep records that prove that you are making a profit. Don't get stuck in your competition's lower pricing. Charge what you are worth and don't apologize for it.

I still have the letter that started this story. It's my reminder that many more people are involved in how you manage your money (especially when you get it wrong) than you think. It's a reminder that business owners have obligations and responsibilities that can't be ignored without consequences. It's a reminder that those of us with families must be mindful of our responsibilities in that area, too. I had put my family in a precarious position of debt. My former business was on the brink of failure because of that same debt. Now? I've learned. I decided to turn around and share my experience, my expertise with the IRS as an IRS-trained Enrolled Agent (EA), and my knowledge of tax law with my clients.

I had to rescue myself from drowning in debt first. I had to pull my family's finances out of danger first.

Now, I rescue clients who are drowning in IRS debt by throwing them a lifeline and pulling them to safety. I know that they need breathing room, and I know what actions they need to take. I help them set up a plan that will get them tax-compliant and debt-free again. I show them money-management tools that will keep them debt-free and compliant with their taxes.

If you owe back taxes, penalties, and interest to the federal government, or you have an IRS lien against your property, you need to keep reading our book.

I'm Kevin Roberts. I'm the Tax Relief Lifeguard. It's my mission to save people from drowning in tax debt.

CHAPTER 4

UNDERSTANDING THE IRS RISK TO YOU AND YOUR BUSINESS

The IRS is the government's go-to tax collector. I discovered that through my SBA loan default situation. The IRS is not just one office. Let me give you a quick overview.

The IRS is a bureau of the US Department of the Treasury. The bureau sets tax administration policy. It is responsible for taxpayer services (answering your questions on their hotline or reviewing your appeals). As most of you know, the IRS also enforces the Internal Revenue Code.

This really means they are a *collection agency*. To perform that work, they divide their taxpayer-facing personnel into four departments. Each focuses on a type of earning segment:

1. Large Business & International (LB&I)

2. Small Business / Self-Employed (SB/SE)

3. Taxpayer Services (TS) (Formerly Wage & Investment)

4. Tax-Exempt & Government Entities (TE/GE)

The bureau additionally has a number of "offices" specializing in appeals, whistleblower claims, or criminal investigations.

How did the IRS get involved in my SBA loan default? An SBA loan is a *federal government* lending program for small businesses. Defaults on SBA loans are funneled through the US Treasury's centralized debt collection system. When Treasury received it, it sent my federal debt for collection to the IRS.

Ignoring your obligations as a taxpayer (or as a federal debtor of any kind) doesn't pose just one risk. The risk that comes to most people's minds first is jail. Rest easy. That is not one of the top risks for most delinquent taxpayers.

The top risks that should come to mind are much different from jail time. Ignoring your tax obligations is a risk to your *money*. Ignoring the tax man is a risk to your *reputation*. Ignoring the IRS puts your *peace of mind* in jeopardy. Ignoring your responsibilities around tax debt could jeopardize your *marriage.* Ignoring your responsibilities around tax debt might just jeopardize your *business partnership.*

The bottom line? Don't ignore the IRS at any time. It's just not worth it.

The Risks You Take with a Tax Debt

Around *3 percent of taxpayers attempting to contact the IRS in 2021 were successful.*[5] More specifically, those taxpayers were attempting to get through to the main *individual income tax* (1040) hotline and talk with an IRS representative.

That sounds like a pitiful success rate, and it is. What's underneath that 97 percent failure rate? First, just having the line connect you to an agent is problematic and has been for many years.[6] Second, once you have an agent on the line, most taxpayers don't know what to say or ask about their 1040 filing.

Also, as of February 2026, staff from the Human Resources (HR) and IT departments have been reassigned to Taxpayer Services. Their duties include customer service representatives, handling taxpayer inquiries, and tax

5 https://www.washingtonpost.com/business/2021/07/02/getting-real-person-at-irs/

6 How hard is it to reach an IRS hotline agent on the 1040 line? The answer is in this Taxpayer Advocate Service article of January 2023, "Most Serious Problem #4: Telephone And In-Person Service. Taxpayers Continue to Experience Difficulties and Frustration Obtaining Telephone and Face-to-Face Assistance to Resolve Their Tax Issues and Questions," https://www.taxpayeradvocate.irs.gov/wp-content/uploads/2023/01/ARC22_MSP_04_Telephone.pdf. Accessed December 2025.

examiners, responsible for reviewing the accuracy of the incoming returns.[7]

Consider this seriously. If you are successful in connecting and speaking with the IRS, do you know what to say? You probably just give the IRS agent on the hotline your spontaneous answers to their questions. But is it fuel for them or for you? Be very careful. Your words matter.

Risk #1: DIY

This brings us to the first, well-hidden risk you take. It is *trying to resolve your tax problems yourself*, with no information about how to go about it.

Do *not* call the IRS hotline. The very first thing you should do to eliminate this risk is to consult a tax resolution professional.

Related to this is the risk of complexity. Do not DIY your taxes when they are very complex or involve multiple years. Do not DIY your taxes when you don't understand the types of information or numbers that are required. This is one very, very common way people get into tax trouble, and don't even realize the risk. They just think, "Why pay H&R Block $400 or more when I can do this? I'm going to save a tax preparation fee."

---

7 Jory Heckman, "IRS officially puts back-office employees on 'involuntary' details to handle filing season work," *Federal News Network*, February 9, 2026, https://federalnewsnetwork.com/workforce/2026/02/irs-officially-puts-back-office-employees-on-involuntary-details-to-handle-filing-season-work/.

A widow contacted me, confused about her tax picture. She'd gotten a letter from the IRS stating that she owed $260,000 for three years of back taxes. She couldn't understand why; she had filed for those years.

Her late husband was a professional athlete. After his death, and for whatever reason (and by the time the IRS catches up to you, the reasons or excuses don't matter anymore), this widow filed on her own. You would think someone like that would have a professional tax preparer at the very least. But this widow filed by herself, without any consultations. By definition, doing taxes in the year of a spouse's death is complicated. She got it wrong that first year and for two more years. On top of that, she didn't know that "filing" and "paying" are two different things.

Of course, I couldn't answer any of her concerns until I obtained the filings for those three years. She'd gotten a lot of her numbers wrong on the forms; she outright forgot others. I corrected everything based on backup documents that I asked for and did an analysis of her situation. She had all that backup and didn't know what to do with it. I did.

I refiled what is called an *amended return* for each year. The IRS accepted the amendments along with the backup documents that the client and I could provide. Instead of *owing* $260,000 in taxes as those IRS letters had indicated, she *received a refund* of $360,000!

Yes, you read that correctly. No, this wasn't instant. It took the IRS about a year. There is another great piece to this story: This widow received the refund check for $360,000 dated December 25—a very, very nice Christmas gift!

The first lesson here is that filing is not the same as filing *and* paying. The second lesson is that taxes are complicated enough that you don't want to DIY them. You need expert help getting all the numbers right.

Risk #2: The Levy

How your problem often starts is that you ignore those IRS letters (and more on them coming up). I know that all too well from personal experience.

When you've ignored them long enough, the IRS implements its first tool for getting paid. This tool is a risk to you. Oh, they tell you it's coming. The problem is that you're not reading the letters that tell you it's coming.

This second financial risk is a *levy*. It applies to salaried individuals, businesses, the self-employed, and even those collecting Social Security. So, what is a levy?

Here is the IRS definition:

> *"An IRS levy is a legal seizure of your property to satisfy a tax debt. It can garnish wages, take money in your bank or other financial account, seize and sell your vehicle(s), real estate, and other personal property."*[8]

8 The IRS levy authority and its process: https://www.irs.gov/businesses/small-businesses-self-employed/what-is-a-levy. Accessed December 2025.

Not only this, the IRS can levy municipalities and states that might owe you a *tax refund.* They levy your accounts with those authorities. The IRS essentially orders them to, "Send the refund to us, not the taxpayer. They have a federal tax debt to clear."[9]

In short, the IRS can legitimately levy—seize—money in your bank account and levy funds from your paycheck before the employer can pay it over to you.

Businesses

For a levy on your business bank account, the IRS will take all the funds in that account on the specific day named in their seizure letter to your bank. The bank must, by law, hold that money for the IRS for at least twenty-one days, called a "twenty-one-day hold." If you don't get in touch with the IRS before the end of the hold, the bank will send that levied amount to the IRS after the twenty-one days have expired.

This means you have twenty-one days to talk to the IRS. Since a levy starts with a hold (and not yet a seizure), you can negotiate with the bank to release the hold before the twenty-one days are up. But to achieve that, you first have to have your payment agreement in writing with the IRS. Therefore, your best action is to get in touch right away with a tax resolution expert and hire them to represent you to the IRS.

9 The IRS has two levy programs: https://www.irs.gov/help/irs-levy-programs-toolkit. Accessed December 2025.

Don't blame the bank! The bank is in the hot seat by law to respect that hold, that levy. Their hands are tied.

Let me comfort you, though. The levy is just for that one day shown in the letter. Whatever amount is in that bank account on that one day, they'll take it out and hold it for the IRS. However, if any amount of money gets deposited the next day or thereafter, that amount is not subject to the levy. It will still be there in the bank account, available to you to withdraw at any time. Stated differently, if the IRS levies your bank account on May 1, when you have $10,000 in the account, that $10,000 is gone. On May 2, May 3, etc., if more deposits are made, those appear as available to the account holder.

Let me tell you a story about a business in trouble. I might not have mentioned that 80 percent of my tax resolution business is with individual taxpayers. But as I was drafting this chapter, I got a disturbing call from a corporate client. They are a healthcare company, and a levy had been implemented on them the day before. The IRS letter announced the business was subject to a bank account levy. That announcement came after a number of other IRS letters they had already received and ignored. When you arrive at the point of being levied, it's never just after one letter.

No business likes to hear that they are being levied. That could mean that their employees are not going to be paid. It means the company's tax delinquency could go public. Employees know, panic, and talk. Don't get me started on going viral over social media!

It's true: A tax debt at the company level can and does have a whole trickle-down effect on many individuals. This healthcare company brings in around a million dollars per month. They had not filed or paid their taxes for the prior eight years. They had not been paying payroll taxes—not paying employment taxes *for eight years*. The business wouldn't be able to meet their next payroll due to the levy.

For businesses, there is something called a *trust fund.* When you are an employee, your employer pays FICA (a.k.a. the employment or payroll tax) for you. They pay half, and then you, the employee, pay half. You see that line item on every paystub, and the employer's share goes into that trust fund. Across the USA, employees count on the company actually paying their share into the trust fund.

The IRS expects the employer to transfer payroll taxes to it on behalf of its employees, according to a strict payment schedule. The healthcare company hadn't paid into the trust fund as required by law for all those years. It seems like a long time for the IRS to wait, but that is a story for another book!

In the end, the company was just exploring its options through our brief period of consultations. I got a fair amount of information from them. They didn't want to hire me after all. I hope they hired a true specialist, though, because they would never be able to DIY their way out of that debt!

You must be aware that in such a case as I have described, it is most likely that the revenue officer will be very aggressive. In this kind of case, an IRS revenue officer is specifically assigned to follow the case from start to end.

The lesson for business owners is to never procrastinate! It's going to turn into a criminal case. You'll be in court. It will cost you a lot more to settle if it goes that far than to take early action with a tax resolution professional like me. Don't get me started on how much you'll be paying in attorney fees if it comes to that.

There are many related risks here. Your business reputation will be shredded. Your employees will sue. Your clients will flee. Your executives will have a hard time finding new employment if they are perceived to be dishonest conspirators in your tax problems. Banks may never lend to you again, even if you launch a new business. Don't let it get this far.

Individuals

Individuals are not off the hook because they have a related risk: the IRS *paycheck or wage levy*. This doesn't go through your bank, but through your employer. The IRS will contact your employer by letter and let them know that a portion of So-and-So's paycheck will be garnished. The employer (much like the banks I mentioned above) is in the hot seat and must, by law, withhold the amount indicated and forward it to the IRS.

This is a "wage levy" or "IRS wage garnishment" off the top of their paycheck. Elesha has told you something about the fallout such a garnishment represents. For my part, here is what the IRS states:

> *"If the IRS levies (seizes) your wages, part of your wages will be sent to the IRS each pay period until:*
>
> - *You make other arrangements to pay your overdue taxes,*
> - *The amount of overdue taxes you owe is paid, or*
> - *The levy is released.*
>
> *Part of your wages may be exempt from the levy and the exempt amount will be paid to you. The exempt amount is based on the standard deduction and an "amount determined" calculated in part based on the number of dependents you are allowed for the year the levy is served."*[10]

You usually have a certain number of days to get into some type of agreement with the IRS. If you don't have an agreement with the IRS by that time, the IRS will continue to garnish you; your next paychecks are at risk. They'll leave a certain percentage just for living expenses. For instance, if you make $1,000 per check, the IRS might

10 Wage levies or garnishments: https://www.irs.gov/businesses/small-businesses-self-employed/information-about-wage-levies. Accessed January 2026.

leave you only $200 in your paycheck instead of that whole thousand dollars.

This can be embarrassing. The payroll staff at your company knows you have a tax debt. But don't go yelling at the payroll team or the owner of your company—they are obligated by federal law to follow the IRS's instructions here. It's not their fault. They are being compliant with the law (and if not, the company itself is penalized).

The fallout can go beyond you needing to "tighten your belt" when it comes to covering your bills. It can and does affect your family's emotional, mental, and physical health and well-being. I actually, and very unfortunately, put my wife, Elesha, through a paycheck garnishment. It was because of my debt, but we were legally married, and thus the IRS could and did go after her paycheck. Don't doubt that the IRS is in its legal right to go after spousal earnings even when it was the other spouse who was delinquent.

The lesson here is that it is always smart to get ahead of the debt by consulting with a tax resolution professional like me. Do so the moment you get that first letter from the IRS. Don't let more letters arrive and more time go by. Garnishment is no laughing matter, and you can avoid it.

Risk #3: Security Clearance Revocation

The third risk is indirectly financial. The risk is that the IRS may *levy your security clearance*. This primarily applies to military or federal workers, or your profession as a government contractor. This security clearance levy or block can be legally implemented when you have an IRS debt that you never paid on.

For many, a security clearance is required to perform the work that earns their income. Your security clearance is at risk if you have ignored your tax obligations. Your clearance can be revoked or downgraded if you have a tax debt and have been ignoring the IRS to resolve it. If you were eligible for a clearance upgrade, the upgrade approval might be blocked.

If you are trying to get a high-grade security clearance, the government will be looking into your records. They want to see that you are in compliance with the IRS. This would include timely filing of tax returns or a balance due on a past tax debt. If you are in a repayment agreement, they want to see that you're making payments as agreed.

If you haven't arranged a payment plan with the IRS and have not been in touch with the IRS, you are considered delinquent. Blocking or revoking your clearance is one of the ways they get your attention.

The lesson? If you are in the running for an upgraded security or any other type of clearance, make sure you are tax-compliant. When the employing agency discovers you have an IRS debt with no plan or agreement in place to resolve it, issuance of a first security clearance or approval of your upgrade would be blocked.

I received an industry letter recently about the number of military and federal employees who are not current with their taxes. Around 525,000 current and retired federal employees are receiving IRS letters because they are not in tax compliance. Note that there are 2.8 million current federal employees, plus 2.7 million retired federal employees, for a total of 5.5 million federal employees.

This means that *one out of ten federal employees* has a tax debt! Now, not all of those noncompliant federal employees have a security clearance; that retiree population probably doesn't care much about their prior clearances. But those who are currently employed are risking their jobs, aren't they? Here is what the IRS notification looks like when a federal employee (one of my clients) is delinquent:

IRS

Department of the Treasury
Internal Revenue Service
ACS Support
P.O. Box 24017
Fresno, CA 93779-4017

Time Sensitive Information - Open Immediately

June 23, 2025

Urgent: You have an outstanding tax issue

According to our records, you are one of approximately 525,000 current or retired federal employees who are noncompliant with respect to their federal tax obligations as of April 30, 2025. We appreciate your service to the Government and dedication to supporting the United States.

As you know, everyone has a responsibility to pay their taxes on a timely basis and current or retired federal employees should also lead by example. We expect you to resolve this matter promptly. You can call a service center employee at 800-829-7650. Please understand that we will follow up with you directly if these obligations are not timely resolved.

Congress has mandated that federal employees serve as stewards of the law and under 5 C.F.R. § 2635, federal employees "shall satisfy in good faith their obligations as citizens, including all just financial obligations, especially those—such as Federal, State, or local taxes—that are imposed

Risk #4: Passport Revocation

The fourth risk is to your freedom of movement. *Your passport can be revoked.* It can be revoked here at home, whether or not you have pending overseas travel. Your passport can (and this should frighten you) be revoked while you are overseas, allowing only an immediate return to the United States.

The IRS works in tandem with the US Department of State, which issues all passports. Here is what the IRS states about this risk:

> *"By law,[11] the IRS will certify taxpayers with seriously delinquent tax debts to the State Department for specific actions regarding their passports.*
>
> *"Generally, the State Department will not issue passports to taxpayers after receiving their delinquent debt certification from the IRS. The State Department may also deny a taxpayer's passport application or revoke their current passport.*
>
> *"If taxpayers with certified tax debts are overseas, the State Department may issue a limited-validity passport allowing the taxpayer to return directly to the United States.*

11 Internal Revenue Bulletin: 2018-3, January 16, 2018, https://www.irs.gov/irb/2018-03_IRB#NOT-2018-01. Accessed December 2025.

> *"What are seriously delinquent tax debts?*
>
> *"Seriously delinquent tax debts are legally enforceable, unpaid federal tax debt (including assessed penalties and interest) totaling more than $64,000 (adjusted yearly for inflation)."*[12]

The IRS certifies a seriously delinquent tax debt (meaning more than $64,000 in back taxes) and reports that to the Department of State. If that debt threshold is met or exceeded, you will likely not be able to get your passport renewed. Note that the IRS only reports you to the Department of State as a matter of procedure; they don't know whether or not you hold a passport.

It is then that the Department of State has discretionary action. When you try to apply for a first passport or renew one you hold, the Department of State will make a decision. It can deny new passports, refuse to renew your passport, outright revoke a current passport, or limit the passport's access (limit the countries you may enter with it).

Usually, as long as you still have an active passport, you may travel as you wish. That is because, even though you might be seriously delinquent, as long as the passport hasn't expired, you may (typically, not always) use it for travel.

---

12 https://www.irs.gov/businesses/small-businesses-self-employed/revocation-or-denial-of-passport-in-cases-of-certain-unpaid-taxes. Accessed December 2025.

Take this as very general information, as the Department of State is the final authority on limiting your passport.

The lesson here is that if you travel abroad a lot, you have one way that you can avoid or reverse this IRS certification of tax debt statement to the US Department of State: Resolve your debt!

In a nutshell, if you want freedom to travel, the certification has to be lifted. The State Department has the flag on you from the IRS, but it is the IRS you talk to. Get in touch with the IRS, preferably through me (remember my warnings about DIY risks). To be eligible to lift this levy, you must, of course, pay your full tax debt. Renewing your passport afterward can still take up to several months.

There are other risks associated with your federal tax debt that can directly affect your life and living. They are the risks you must watch out for in your actions. On its side of the table, the IRS is watching too. They are looking for red flags you may not even know you are waving. Let's look at those next.

CHAPTER 5

RED FLAGS THE IRS WATCHES FOR

Don't ignore your obligations. Don't avoid your responsibilities. You run a risk of IRS action against you or your business because you have somehow waved a bright red flag in their face. In other words, you have broken some rule.

I told the healthcare company story in the previous chapter. Not paying payroll taxes for that many years is always, always a big IRS red flag that could eventually become a criminal case.

Don't wave any flags! Some lead to letters being sent to you. Others lead to audits. Some lead to the IRS marking your account for more observation. Some lead to investigations into criminal fraud. Don't wave these red flags.

The Most Common Flags

First, just accept your obligations and responsibilities and follow through. Every quarter, every year, your business has filing and payment obligations to the IRS. Every year, the IRS is watching for your filing that declares your personal income and your payment of taxes due.

That's basic. Don't ignore those obligations. Next, know what else the IRS is watching for. Here are some of the typical errors I see in my work that are red flags to the IRS:

1. Claiming too many deductions on the tax return. The rule is simple: Do not claim deductions that you are not eligible for. If in doubt, why aren't you consulting an expert tax preparer?

2. Claiming too many business expenses. Do not claim amounts that exceed the average for your business industry unless you have ironclad backup (receipts and documented justification for the expense). If in doubt, consult an expert tax preparer with experience in your industry.

3. Failing to file tax returns. This applies to individuals and businesses. This is about sending in that form or set of forms. Not filing is a red flag any time, but especially when your income is substantial.

4. Omitting, misreporting, or understating income on your tax forms. The IRS has multiple ways of verifying the business or personal income numbers on your tax forms. All income, from all sources, and paid to you by all media (cash, check, digital transfers) must be reported. Whether you earned income through an owned business, a salaried/hourly wage position, or independent contracting work, file the correct amounts. If you earned cash, declare it.

5. Misunderstanding or abusing extensions. This is often due to a misunderstanding of what an extension is. All payments are due by April 15. Extensions refer to the time to file the paperwork supporting the payment you made in April. You also have to request an extension. It is not automatic. Note that if you are late paying (i.e., after April 15), you will have late-payment penalties. To avoid this becoming a red flag, pay your best estimated federal tax by April 15. Respect the paperwork filing extension deadline.

Common IRS Letters

I'm going to do some deeper show-and-tell in Chapter 8 around IRS letters, because they each have a different purpose. However, their number one shared purpose is to get you to communicate with the IRS, to take remedial action—to do something! As Elesha explained, they are intentionally worded to motivate you to take a certain action.

We pay our taxes with a check made out to the "US Department of the Treasury." However, the letters I speak of in Chapter 5 will come from the Internal Revenue Service, not from the Treasury. Pay attention to any letter from the Internal Revenue Service! The IRS has a reputation. People are afraid of the IRS. As Elesha has told you, that is *intentional.* Those letters are *intentionally* scary.

Here is your #1 rule of thumb:

> When you receive a letter from the IRS, you need to open it and address the issue. *Immediately* address the issue. In other words, do what the letter tells you to do.

Here is your #2 rule of thumb:

> When you don't understand what the letter means or what it is asking you to do, *seek professional advice.* Do not call the IRS hotline. *Immediately* seek out an expert's advice. Come to me. I'll explain the letter.

In both those cases, this is crucial: *Act immediately.* Do not let one day go by. Take action. Or, in case of need, get that professional direction. Why do I pound this so hard? Almost every IRS letter gives you a time frame in which to respond. Non-response within that time frame will tell the IRS to escalate.

When I had the tax preparation business, clients I saw only once a year would come in at tax time with several IRS letters they had *not even opened*. They had waited sometimes a whole year to even open the letters. Don't do that. The reason those clients had several letters is that the IRS didn't hear from them. So they wrote again. And again. The IRS escalated.

Not responding to letters you receive makes it very difficult to resolve your issue. I can sympathize with getting six or seven letters that you avoid reading or acting on. Been there, done that. Don't! With every new letter, you are falling far behind in your ability to resolve your debt. With every new letter, the cost—the actual dollar cost—of not taking action increases.

Tax Preparation Is Not Tax Resolution

Another issue that I have seen is when an individual or a business uses a tax firm that only prepares current-year taxes. They are not in the tax resolution business at all. Tax preparation and filing is a very different profession from tax debt resolution. If you bring your IRS letters to your tax preparer during tax season, they are swamped, and there are two problems right away.

First, they will say, "Let's wait until tax season dies down, and then we'll address the issue." It might be too late. It will *probably* be too late.

Second, they are not in the tax debt resolution business. Some of them don't know how to properly deal with the IRS or properly resolve your tax debt. They won't be able to officially represent you to the IRS as an IRS Enrolled Agent (an EA) can.

That's the reason I chose the tax *resolution* business. When those letters come in, when clients receive those letters, we address them right then and there. I don't prepare or file current-year taxes at all anymore. I never have to say, "Let's wait till after tax season." Tax resolution happens every day at my office.

Just this week, on one October Monday, I received twenty-five letters from the IRS for my clients. Since I am their recognized representative (EA) to the IRS, those letters now arrive at my office, not their homes or offices. I deal with them all when they arrive—no waiting. This means I'm in touch with each client, but also with the IRS on their behalf.

Pay attention to any letter from the Internal Revenue Service!

Even though you filed and paid what was calculated on your forms, you might get an IRS letter six months later. That could be because they didn't agree with your calculation, and they say, "Oh no, Taxpayer. You got it wrong. According to our calculations and research, you need to pay us more. Here is our number." They might be writing to say, "Hey, you filed, but you did not pay the declared amount of taxes (or the whole amount)." Whatever the IRS letter says, bring it to me immediately. You need to act so that the IRS collection actions pause and so you can avoid penalties and interest on taxes they say that you owe.

About That Pause

When Elesha's check was garnished, I scrambled to take action (yes, finally). When I got in touch with the IRS a couple of weeks later, the very fact of being in touch with them about my SBA default paused all further garnishments. An IRS *pause* means that they will stop all collection actions because you have been in touch to arrange a solution.

That is why it is important to take immediate action when you get an IRS notification. I was able to stop the garnishment action for good by taking the action the IRS approved (more on that later).

How Penalties and Interest Work

The IRS may state in some of its later letters to you that you have a penalty to pay. There are various types of penalties that the IRS can impose. It may be for a *Failure to File*, a *Failure to Pay*, or an *Accuracy-Related Penalty.*

Failure to File Penalty

The Failure to File penalty is 5 percent each month, increasing as the months go by to a maximum of 25 percent monthly for the duration of the debt. The penalties accrue every single month that your debt is not paid in full.

Failure to Pay Penalty

Failure to pay is penalized in the same amounts as above. You can be subject to both penalties if you neither paid nor filed. It effectively doubles your penalties every month.

People think just because they filed for an extension, they won't accrue any penalties. They filed for an extension, but they did not pay by April 15. They will not have a Failure to File penalty, and that is true because they are in compliance with that requirement. But they will have a Failure to Pay penalty because they didn't pay even an estimated amount on time.

April 15 is a hard-and-fast *payment* deadline. All payments are due whether you actually sent in the supporting paperwork (the 1040 or whatever tax forms you file).

Accuracy-Related/Understated Income Penalty

This is a penalty for not stating all your income on your tax form. It might be due to negligence or disregard of the rules. Whether intentionally or unintentionally understating your income to the IRS, you are penalized for the inaccuracy.

Do not doubt this fact: The IRS has many, many ways to double-check your tax return for accurate, complete statements of income. Employers send to the IRS information that is compared to your return. They can review your credit card and bank statements and contact state tax authorities about your status.

In the case of a "substantial understatement of income," the IRS assesses a penalty equal to 20 percent of the unstated income. Negligence or disregard for the rules falls under accuracy-related infractions. The keys here are 1) correct and 2) complete. If not, you risk penalties for "substantial understatement of income."

Stated differently, if the total amount of income the IRS has on record for you is $25,000, but you only reported $20,000, you understated $5,000. The 20 percent penalty is levied on that $5,000.

The IRS states it this way:

> *How we calculate the penalty:*
>
> *The penalty is 5% of the tax due (less any tax paid on time and available credits) for each month or partial month the return is late. The penalty accrues up to a maximum of 25%.*
>
> *We calculate the failure to file penalty in this way:*
> - *Tax required to be shown on the return,*
> - *Less any tax paid on time (example: withholding credits or estimated tax payments),*
> - *Less available refundable credits, then*
> - *Multiplied by 5% per month (up to 25%).*
>
> *If the return is more than 60 days late, the minimum penalty is the amount listed or 100% of the underpayment, whichever is less.*[13]

13 Penalties are defined on the irs.gov website here: https://www.irs.gov/payments/penalties. Accessed December 2025.

What Is a Penalty Abatement?

A client came to me with a Failure to File problem. My client had paid taxes in full and on time, but without filing the forms. The IRS considered the amount paid to be the full payment due, so that was in his favor.

Still, the IRS informed him that he owed $115,000 in penalties alone, due to his failure to file. For every month he did not file the forms, the penalties increased. You don't want to pay 25 percent of your tax-due amount just because you are too lazy to get the forms completed and sent in. Don't assume that just because the IRS has your money, you are in the clear.

This Failure to File scenario seems backward to a lot of people. My client paid in full and on time. He did not file his tax return *form* at all. This backward scenario happens a lot, however, because taxpayers are pinched for time to focus on the paperwork (those tax forms) and believe that the IRS is only really interested in the money. Not so. The IRS levies penalties when you ignore all or even part of your obligations. They want those forms too.

More is at risk for you in this case than the current year's taxes alone. When they spot a current-year problem, the IRS looks at your past three years for compliance in filing and paying. If you were compliant all three years—and in this client's case, he was—you are eligible for an *abatement* (or reduction) of those penalty amounts. The IRS will never guarantee a 100 percent abatement, but it is common.

Penalties and More

I haven't mentioned *interest*, but keep in mind that you are not just being charged that penalty amount. You are also charged the interest accruing on your past-due taxes and on the penalty amount.[14] Interest is rarely abated or waived. The interest rate equals the federal short-term rate plus three percentage points for individuals, compounded daily, and is reset every calendar quarter.

Back to my Failure to File client: In his case, although he had paid a correct amount of income tax, he still owed $115,000 in penalties alone. Add the interest, which was up to $45,000 by then. However, given the history of compliant payments and prior-year filings by my client, the entire amount of interest was fully wiped out. The total cleared amount for penalties and interest that I obtained for this client was $160,000.

Though I mainly talk to individual taxpayers in my tax resolution work, I do advise and assist business owners. You must protect your business. You must protect your staff. Get compliant and remain in compliance with the IRS.

If the IRS writes to you at your business, pay attention and take action. If you're not taking care of the requests in their letters, you are at risk of losing the business. You are at risk of not having the funds to cover payroll (remember levies). You will end up having more debts than taxes alone.

14 Interest begins on the original due date of the return (typically April 15) until the balance is paid in full. https://www.irs.gov/payments/quarterly-interest-rates. Accessed December 2025.

CHAPTER 6

BUSINESSES, BEWARE OF MISCLASSIFICATIONS

Let me present two cases for all taxpayers to become aware of.

First case: You're a business owner and you employ people. The top red flag that brings the IRS to your business's door is payroll tax mistakes.

Second case: You work for one or more businesses. If a business has misclassified the type of worker you are, it might be why you have a tax debt.

Worker Classifications

Whether your business is paying the worker or you are the worker who is paid, there are IRS rules around payroll tax calculation and payment. Those taxes are due quarterly, so the IRS will very quickly know whether your business is or is not paying them and submitting the right paperwork. There's an associated risk for businesses: *not paying those taxes on all the workers you should be counting.*

Everyone who has earned a salary has heard of a W-2. Similarly, if you are self-employed, you know about a 1099 (and keep reading if you don't). Forms W-2 and 1099 are two different ways of not only receiving but also legally recording payment for work performed. They are called "worker classifications" and are not interchangeable.

W-2 Employees

These are people "on the payroll" who may be full-time or part-time workers. Here are the rules for determining whether a worker *must be on the payroll*:

- The employer controls the work and the work hours.
  - Employers (managers, supervisors) provide direction and supervision.
  - The company sets mandatory work hours/schedules.

- The employer supplies all the tools, such as workspace, software, hardware, and all equipment needed to perform the work safely and fully.

- The employer expects you to show up as scheduled and use the supplied resources and spaces.

- The employer withholds and pays the business's share of payroll taxes (FICA, or Social Security and Medicare; FUTA, or federal unemployment tax).

- The employer must respect rules around benefits in their industry and/or state.

1099 Contractors

These are self-employed individuals. They are also called *independent contractors* (IC) or 1099 workers. Employers typically hire them for specific tasks or projects. The collaboration might be short-term or longer. Here are the rules for determining whether a worker is an *independent contractor*:

- The IC controls their own work methods and schedule.
  - » The employing company may not and does not control work methods or impose work schedules on any independent contractor.
  - » When and how the IC works is the independent choice of the contractor. The only guideline is to produce the promised work within the promised time frame.

- The IC must subscribe to their own benefits (or not, as they wish).

  - » The employing company does not provide benefits—there is no requirement to do so.

- The IC is required to report all income from such work and pay all FICA and self-employment taxes.
  - » The employer will not withhold taxes from the IC's pay. The IC is responsible for their own tax liability.

- The IC invoices the business for work performed.
  - » The business pays that net amount to the IC (with no withholding done).

Those are the main differences. And by the way, claiming ignorance of the differences is not a valid excuse for any taxpayer when the IRS shows up at your door.

There are other criteria around taxes and benefits to determine how you are classified.

When you are a W-2 employee

As an employee, you pay a portion of your paycheck toward your income taxes, and another portion toward FICA, which is Social Security and Medicare. This is called *withholding*—the employer withholds it from your paycheck. Your portion of FICA is 7.65% of your pay. Your employer pays that same amount for a total of 15.3% paid into your tax account. You know this because it appears on your pay stub or statement at every pay period.

When you are a W-2 employee, your company may offer (and pay for) benefits. Your company, if large enough, offers a retirement plan you can opt into. The W-2 employee cannot itemize and deduct expenses when filing taxes.

When you are a 1099 worker

As an independent contractor, you don't receive a paycheck or a pay stub. At the end of your project, you bill the employer and get paid a previous agreed-upon amount, perhaps with a check stub or other record of which invoice is being paid. This company doesn't offer you any benefits or a retirement plan. They just pay you the money you charged them for the agreed work. At the end of a tax year, you get a Form 1099 from each company you invoiced more than $600.

As far as the FICA goes, you pay the entire amount on your own through your tax return (Schedule SE). It is 12.4% of your earnings for Social Security plus 2.9% of your earnings for Medicare, or the whole 15.3% (often called the professional tax). The 1099 contractor can itemize and deduct allowed expenses from gross income earned. Those expenses must be "ordinary and necessary for business" expenses and backed up by receipts.

In short, there are clear distinctions between these two classes of workers. IRS uses a "common-law" test.[15] It is focused on behavioral and financial *control,* and the

15 Independent contractor (self-employed) or employee? https://www.irs.gov/businesses/small-businesses-self-employed/independent-contractor-self-employed-or-employee. Accessed December 2025.

type of *relationship* between your business and the worker. When there is a red flag, the IRS will get answers to these questions:

1. Who controls how the work is done?
2. Who controls the business and financial aspects of the work?
3. What is the nature of the business relationship?

If the business controls the worker, the worker is a W-2 employee. If the worker controls the work, the worker is a self-employed individual who receives a 1099.

When I'm speaking to a group, I have some fun and ask, "How many of you are 1099 employees?" About 75 percent raise their hands. This is my *Gotcha!* moment because there's no such thing as a "1099 employee." You are a 1099 *contractor.* Otherwise, you are a payrolled *employee.*

Note that the IRS is always very curious to know how every business is paying workers.[16] They want to know under what sort of management or control workers function. They'll find out when employers are paying a controlled employee as an *independent contractor.* If this employer is you, then you are out of compliance. You should be paying

16 IC or W-2? https://www.irs.gov/newsroom/worker-classification-101-employee-or-independent-contractor. Accessed December 2025.

the workers as W-2 employees. If not, your business is in hot water.

Penalties for Misclassifying Workers

Let me come back to the painful topic of penalties. I'll start with two pieces of bad news.

1. Whether deliberate or negligent, the IRS will catch you in misclassifying your workers.

2. Misclassification costs you big money.

Have no doubt: However it is brought to their attention, the IRS will research this issue. Misclassifying workers, whether intentional or accidental, will not go unnoticed. It will cost your business quite a lot. The IRS-imposed penalties are not a business expense you want or need.

The main reason an employer intentionally misclassifies its workers is money, of course. The employer may not make enough money to cover the payroll expenses. Perhaps the employer just doesn't want to pay.

Unintentional, Non-Willful Misclassification

If the IRS concludes that the misclassification was *an honest mistake*, penalties are still assessed. They are detailed under 26 U.S. Code § 3509, "Determination of employer's liability for certain employment taxes."[17] These penalties are:

17 About payroll taxes and worker classification: https://www.irs.gov/pub/irs-drop/rr-25-03.pdf. Accessed December 2025.

- Failure to File Information Returns (W-2s): This assesses a penalty of $50 per missing Form W-2 that should have been filed.

- Unpaid Income Tax Withholding: This assesses a penalty equal to 1.5 percent of the wages paid to the misclassified worker.

- Employee's Share of FICA Taxes (Social Security and Medicare): This assesses a penalty of 20 percent of the employee's share of FICA taxes that should have been withheld.

- Employer's Share of FICA Taxes: This assesses a penalty of 100 percent of the employer's matching share of FICA taxes (Social Security and Medicare), *plus interest.*

- Failure to Deposit/Pay Penalty: This assesses a general penalty of 0.5 percent per month (up to 25 percent total) on the unpaid tax liability.

Intentional, Willful, Fraudulent Misclassification

The IRS will always do its research. They want to know whether the business knowingly and intentionally misclassified workers to avoid taxes. If yes, the IRS can and does impose penalties far harsher than the amounts I listed above. The penalties may even include criminal charges.

- Increased Wage Penalty: The penalty on wages can rise to (equal) 20 percent of the worker's wages.

- FICA Taxes: This includes 100 percent of both the employer's and the employee's share of FICA taxes, plus interest.

- Criminal Penalties: Intentional misclassification can lead to criminal charges, including:
  - » Fines of up to $1,000 per misclassified worker
  - » Possible employer imprisonment of up to one year

There are those monetary penalties, of course. No business wants that cost. But you also risk an audit of your business's finances. An audit can lead to criminal charges and your imprisonment. If you imagined saving money on payroll taxes, forget it right now. Those fines and interest should wake you up. If applied to even one employee, the amount your business would owe is going to be exorbitant. What if the IRS applied the above penalties to all your employees? What if you had been misclassifying for years? Your business can't afford the past-due withholdings, penalties, interest, and loss of reputation. Pay attention. Classify correctly.

Who Told the IRS?

The IRS knows of the misclassification in one of three main ways.

The first way is that one or more employees has blown the whistle on the employer. A lot of the IRS's information comes from disgruntled, misclassified employees. Workers today are very knowledgeable about the classification difference. They know that they are, in reality, a managed W-2 employee. They have noticed that there was no tax or FICA withholding done. They are frustrated about the denial of professional recognition and promotions due to them. Your workers notice when they are denied benefits. When they aren't paid time off or offered health insurance, a retirement plan, or withholding, they talk. W-2 employees expect the company to do the tax withholding for them. If they get a Form 1099 at year-end, they take it to payroll and discover that no payroll or income taxes have been withheld. If they aren't getting pay stubs or summaries at every pay period, they are suspicious right away. If they are asked to invoice the company (but not always), they will demand to know why. If you've misclassified, count on it: These employees will contact the IRS and report you.

The second way the IRS discovers your misclassification is through their own research capabilities, which includes information sharing amongst federal and state agencies, banks, and financial institutions. Even before the digital age, the IRS had many more resources and research capabilities than you can imagine. Your business is not invisible and never was. Use of digital tools by individuals and businesses just makes lots of IRS research easier. Never assume state tax authorities don't talk to the IRS! The IRS can obtain information from banks. Never assume they won't match your bank deposit statements to your tax return or state filings with federal ones.

The third way the IRS discovers misclassification is when it conducts an audit. The audit may not even be of your business, but through cross-referencing, your business misclassification comes to light.

One last word on how your misclassification pops up on the IRS's radar. Cash. Cash for work is a red flag to the IRS. Cash is not an invisible transaction, contrary to many businesses' and workers' hopes. Cash earnings are taxable! In many of those cases, the employer does not even classify the worker as a 1099 contractor in their recordkeeping or send a 1099 at year-end. The cash worker might also decide not to declare any of the cash earned. I have seen this too many times.

Your business is not invisible.

However the IRS discovers it, the employer is notified by letter about the misclassification.

Small businesses believe they are invisible. Not true. They believe that "they are too small for the IRS to bother with." Not true. The IRS is cracking down on misclassification and non-classification because it wants to (and will) collect all taxes due. Remember that the IRS is above all a collection agency. Remember that it is the collection agency for all federal obligations (FICA and FUTA included).

It never matters if it was a mistake or an intentional act. In this kind of scenario, when you don't correctly classify your workers and pay the right amount of tax and on time, the IRS will come knocking to collect what is owed.

CHAPTER 7

PREVENT AND RESOLVE TAX PROBLEMS

Here I'll be speaking to those with a business of whatever size and to 1099 contractors. 1099 contractors take note, because you are considered by the IRS as a mini-business with tax-reporting obligations.

Attention to your money is vital in business to know whether you are making or losing money. That's basic. Accurate and daily recordkeeping for your business, whatever its size, is key to preventing money- and tax-related problems from occurring. In my personal and now professional experience, accurate and written records are far from common.

First, record everything. If that's in a pen-and-paper ledger that you hand over to an outsourced bookkeeper at the end of every month, do it. If it's in an Excel spreadsheet, do it. If it's in a full-blown business financial management software package, do it. Record everything. Record where the money was spent and for what purpose. Record who paid the money to you and in exchange for what work.

Next, you need to make sure that you separate business money from personal money. Many times, small business owners or independent contractors have only one checking account for all needs. You have combined personal expenses and business expenses—this is called *commingling funds.* When you look at your bank statement, you don't know which expenses are personal and which are business. Have at least two bank accounts. Separate business banking from personal banking.

This brings us back to written recordkeeping. Separate your business's income and expense tracking systems from your personal income and expenses in your records. If you have two or more businesses, each one must be tracked separately from the others and from your personal money.

Recording dollar amounts is not enough. You absolutely want to make sure you track everything on the business side with receipts (both paper and digital). A 1099 worker should track all net income received by using an invoicing system. 1099 workers should track all purchases that support their professional activity by keeping and recording receipts.

Record each source separately. Do not group any receipts or payments; itemize everything.

For example, if Client X pays you an amount every month, record those separately each month, not as an annual lump sum. You must also know where every penny is going when the business pays out money. For example, if you buy from Hardware Store ABC several times a month, record each purchase separately. Get the dated receipt for each purchase. Write the name of the project or client you spent it on. Do not do lump-sum recordkeeping such as "November: $1,482.35 at ABC." Itemize.

I told you that when my wife Elesha's paycheck was garnished, she pretty quickly sat down to separate all our financial accounts. Yes, true. I had not separated accounts, and I should have. Lesson learned. She created "his and hers" accounts and did it by closing joint accounts—and she was right. On my side, I made sure my business money was fully separate from my personal money calculations too.

Leverage Software

How do you keep track of actual invoices and receipts in this digital world? Software.

QuickBooks is a software application that is user-friendly to keep track of everything for any type of business you can name. If not QuickBooks, use some other type of software appropriate to your business. Whichever software tool you select, get a professional to set it up. Do not do it yourself! Get fully trained on it and use it yourself. Use it daily.

Many of the best software applications allow you to take pictures of receipts and upload them so that they are appropriately classified. You can do this with any printed receipts, such as gas or fuel or in-store purchases for the business. There are applications for mileage tracking that are very user-friendly and provide digital or printed records for tax-deduction accuracy.

If you are resistant to buying a full accounting software application, you still have no excuse not to do recordkeeping. I know some 1099 contractors who started with that pen-and-paper system, recording in a bound ledger book that they handed to a bookkeeper and then to their tax preparer. Later, those same people still only used a fairly simple Microsoft Excel spreadsheet. Again, get some training. There are some simple formulas you can set up in Excel that turn a list of numbers into an income/expense dashboard for you.

If you are really not digital, use pen-and-ledger notes that you give to a trained bookkeeper every Monday morning—and keep all your printed and digital receipts. Your bookkeeper is going to turn those numbers and receipts into your official tracking records.

All of my clients come to me with a tax debt or a tax audit to deal with. They all knew that they should have been keeping records. The problem? Like me with my SBA loan default, they procrastinated. They failed to keep records. Many failed (also like me) to separate business from personal money. In my work with clients, I see that many headaches come from commingling funds. My clients only realized the risks of commingling during an IRS audit—when it was too late. In my very painful personal experience, *it's not a lack of knowledge. It's a lack of doing.*

On the IRS side of this, the tax authorities never tell us *how* to keep our records. We choose the method and the tools. Every business person should know this, though:

You must keep exact, truthful records.

If the IRS audits you, you have to show proof that your declared numbers are real. So? Keep accurate records. You need to truthfully record all income from all sources and accurately record all allowed business expenses.

It's not your lack of knowledge.
It's your lack of doing.

Accuracy also means your workers are correctly classified and those payroll tax records are accurate, up-to-the-minute, and paid.

Two Risk-Prevention Tips

There are two ways to protect your business that many businesses ignore.

First, the best way for businesses to prevent tax problems is to *file and pay those quarterly payroll taxes* on correctly classified workers.

Let me say again that this is the top way businesses get into tax debt. You can't put off paying those payroll taxes. You can't be a week late with them. You can't file and not pay. You can't pay and not file. You must, as an employer responsible for your staff's withholdings, follow the rules. This is an issue of trust on the part of your employees. They expect that you will correctly manage payroll taxes and withholdings. Don't break their trust. Don't get into hot water with the IRS.

Second, you get in trouble because of *cash flow management* problems. Just looking at money actually in your bank account is not cash flow management.

If you are a 1099 worker, you are also expected to file and pay estimated FICA on a quarterly basis. Speak to your tax preparer for assistance in doing this. When you don't file and pay quarterly, you are fined. Just like a larger business.

Budgets for Your Business

You need a system (probably digital) so that you know that you can buy that expensive piece of equipment today for your business and still meet all your bills next month and in three months. Spending money you think you have today can put you in the red next month or next quarter.

How do you know? You have to know where your business's money is coming from and when. You have to know what you spend it on and when. You need a tool (and software applications are excellent for this; so is a properly set up Excel worksheet) to show you the ramifications on next month's available cash of spending that money today.

As an example, I set up an Excel worksheet (Elesha will tell you I'm a big fan of Excel!) for a client to demonstrate to him the effects of taking an owner's draw in any month. He saw that taking $10,000 this month (once the spreadsheet updated) would put his cash position in the red two months from now and into the future after that. I let him play with changing the draw amount until he saw how much he could in fact take out of the business that month to pay himself. It turned out that he could safely withdraw $6,000 that month with no negative effects on the business cash position.

This type of planning is Business 101. Like I did years ago, many of my clients fail to plan their money with budgets.

If you fail to plan, you have planned to fail.

A budget helps you plan. A budget tells you how much you make and how much you allow yourself to spend this month.

A well-designed digital budget can project cash flows into the future. You can instantly project the effect of spending $1,000 today on your cash flow three months from now.

A budget also reminds you of the due dates of all invoices. Line items in your budget remind you of your payroll taxes, state sales tax submissions, state and federal income tax due on your business income. You know you must pay those.

Not using a real-time budget and not using a budget to project into the future are why a lot of businesses have cash flow problems. Cash flow problems are probably the top reason businesses fail (I can relate to this one). They spend money they "think" they have because they only look at their bank balance. They have not projected into the future to see how that affects other bills coming up.

Money Rules

Many clients have tax problems because they have not set any financial rules. I learned most of these rules the hard way. Such a set of rules will help your reputation as a serious business. Your employees watch how you manage business matters. So do the tax authorities. So does your bank, your investors, and your silent financial partners. Your business is not invisible, and neither are your processes. Having and following money rules keeps you audit-proof. They allow you to sleep at night in your peaceful home.

Let me summarize some money rules we've already looked at that help businesses manage their money in real time.

1. Keep separate bank and financial accounts for personal and business. If you have more than one business, separate those bank accounts too.

2. Use recordkeeping software. Learn how to use it. If you have more than one business, separate that recordkeeping.

  a. Keep receipts and itemize every expense in your software.
  b. Keep itemized records of every dollar of revenue.

3. Pay all your bills and all your people on time and in full.
  a. Bills include payroll and other taxes.
  b. "On time" means you keep a schedule with deadlines and reminders.

4. Don't use your credit card to run daily operations.

5. Keep a budget. Create it to:
  a. Show how much you will spend this year, month-by-month, and what you will spend it on.
  b. Show the future effects of changes in expenses and income.
  c. Monitor cash flows.

6. Charge enough for your products and services. Increase your prices.
  a. Being competitive doesn't mean you undercut all your competition's prices. Too often, that undercuts your cash flow and your ability to pay the bills from it.

   b. Charging enough allows you to pay yourself a living salary.

7. Have a financial cushion for your business, but also for your household. This is sometimes called an "emergency fund."
   a. It is money that you don't need for ordinary expenses, bills, tax payments, etc.
   b. It is not, however, "mad money" to spend at year-end as you like.
   c. It is your emergency fund for when and if you have less money coming into the business or your household.

Quite often, my clients have not used any money-management rules. They have tax debt, because taxes are the last thing they pay (and don't).

Let me tell you just a little about how we can resolve that debt.

Tax Debt Resolution and Payment Options

I'd just like to insert a word here about the federal government and debt collection.

As we've said, the SBA and the US Department of Education's student loans are federal programs.

That means that the US Department of the Treasury is involved with all federal loan defaults—whether they're SBA or student loans. The US Department of the Treasury has bureaus that specialize in the collection of debt. For defaulted SBA loans, this happens through the Treasury Offset Program (TOP). Once your collection is in the system, it allows the IRS to intercept up to 100 percent of your federal tax refund to pay the overdue loan or tax balance.[18] This aggressive collection extends to other federal payments you are receiving (or expect to receive). Think about Social Security, federal benefits (even administered by states), and so on. Remember that the US Department of the Treasury has broader powers than regular creditors. Thus, under these powers, the US Department of the Treasury can garnish your wages for defaulted federal loans through a process called Administrative Wage Garnishment (AWG) under the Debt Collection Improvement Act of 1996.[19]

On the other side of this coin, when you specifically have a tax debt, the IRS has a number of options or programs to help you resolve your tax debt. I'll discuss just the top three.

Please understand that every taxpayer with a tax debt must first qualify for the option or program. When you owe $10,000 or more, you might have trouble even understanding the options on your own. This is not a DIY activity—come talk to me. You must consult a professional. I have been trained by the IRS in the laws, rules, and

18 Deficit Reduction Act of 1984 (Pub. L. 98369), now codified in Title 26 (IRC) and Title 31 (Money and Finance) of the U.S. Code: 26 U.S.C. 6402 and 31 U.S.C. 3720A.

19 Public Law 104134, section 3100.1.

programs; the IRS has certified me as an Enrolled Agent. I speak their language. I can legally and officially represent you to the IRS.

Unlike the 97 percent of callers who cannot reach an IRS agent, as an EA, my calls to the IRS are taken by priority. Not only that, I know the right questions to ask the agent.

Given my training, I know the best programs to resolve your debt. I will help you determine which option(s) you might qualify for and can stick to. It is not enough to sign an agreement with the IRS—you have to follow through until you are compliant again.

Installment Plans

The first option is an installment plan. There are two common types of installment plans. You are not negotiating the amount due here. In these installment plans, you pay the full amount the IRS has determined is due.

This program allows you to pay off the tax debt by a pre-agreed deadline. You don't have to show any financials. You sign an agreement with the IRS that you can (and must) pay your full debt amount within the stated time frame. The two usual versions of the installment plan are as follows.

The 180-day plan

In this short-term payment agreement, you commit to paying in full within 180 days. It is for taxpayers who owe less than $100,000 in combined back taxes, penalties, and interest. You are signing an agreement to pay it all by the end of the term.

The 72-month plan

This plan gives you six full years to pay the full amount due. It is for taxpayers who owe $50,000 or less (or $25,000 for businesses) in combined back taxes, penalties, and interest. You must have filed all your returns.

There's no monthly amount obligated or pre-set for you by the IRS in either of the above plans. You simply commit to full payment by the end of the term in both these agreements. The following is important to note, as these are conditions of this agreement:

- The interest and the penalties on the outstanding taxes due continue to accrue until the taxes are paid in full.

- The IRS may file a *federal tax lien*[20] on your assets if you owe more than $25,000. The lien is only lifted upon full payment of past-due taxes and continuing compliance in current years. (In the 72-month

20 A lien is the government's legal claim against your property when you neglect or fail to pay a tax debt. The lien protects the government's interest in all your property, including real estate, personal property and financial assets. https://www.irs.gov/businesses/small-businesses-self-employed/understanding-a-federal-tax-lien. Accessed December 2025.

plan, "current" means you must file and pay in full and on time for each of those six years.)

- In case you do not stay current with this and future years' filing and payments, you are considered in default again. A default means that the IRS can and usually will terminate your agreement. In this case, the liens stay in place, your taxes remain due, interest and penalties keep on accruing, and you'll start getting more letters from the IRS.

Partial Pay Installment Agreement (PPIA)

In this resolution program, you have to show financials. The IRS tells you what documentation it requires. To qualify for this program, you must provide every piece of information requested.

Contrary to the previous two plans, the PPIA offers a little bit of a negotiation on the amount of tax due. Your total tax due will be based on what you can afford to pay each month. The monthly payments will typically be small because the IRS wants you to pay every month without fail. The monthly amounts are pre-set (unlike the installment plans).

My role here is to make sure you gather all the required information and to help by calculating how much you can afford. You don't just declare a random number; it must be supported by the provided documentation.

Why is it a "partial pay" agreement? Your smaller monthly payments won't have fully paid your tax debt by the end of the agreement term. The IRS agrees to this, but if you don't stick to the payment agreement—if you default on it—the IRS will expect full payment of the debt.

We call this program the *backdoor route* of getting the offer in compromise. Sometimes your payment is less than it would be with the offer in compromise. Note that this is based on an expiration date and it is a little bit more complicated to qualify for than the payment plans above.

Offer in Compromise

The very first tax-debt-relief program that people hear on the TV and the radio is often this offer in compromise. It is the "pay back less than your full tax debt" that appeals to people, naturally. But it is not that easy to qualify for or negotiate.

This is an option where the IRS agrees that you can settle your debt for less than the full amount owed. The catch: You must qualify according to IRS criteria, which are strict.

To determine whether you are eligible, the IRS collects financial data from you that is beyond just your income. You must provide it, as with the PPIA.

Documented proofs might include your current income, your home value, your mortgage or rent payment amount, mortgages on second homes or investment real estate, your living expenses (amounts and what they are for), all values of motor vehicles you own and loans on them, and other debts or expenses you have, such as alimony or child support. They want to know everything. With this option, you've opened the door to more financial secrets than you might have had to reveal if you had been compliant with your taxes. Failure (or unwillingness) to provide all requested information will probably disqualify you.

This is a difficult—some say impossible—option to pull off on your own. You would have to understand the finer details of the whole process and how it works. When you give your information to the IRS for this program, it can't happen over the phone on their hotline. You have to send them printed financial documents. They're going to look at everything in your life involving money, especially when the tax debt is $10,000 or more. You'll have the IRS writing you requesting more information. You'll have a deadline to respond with whatever they ask for.

Currently Not Collectible (CNC)

What's another way the IRS allows you to resolve? If you can't pay anything without financial hardship, the IRS can temporarily pause collections. Note the keyword here: *pause.*

This is their Currently Not Collectible program (CNC). Note the keyword here: *currently.*

In other words, your debt is not forgiven or forgotten. Not at all. You still have that debt. It will come due. Here, too, you have to provide quite a lot of financial information to the IRS to prove your inability to pay your tax debt. Together with me, you assemble proofs that you only have a reduced amount of income to live on at this time. Remember that it is only a pause in their collection efforts. The taxes remain due, and when you get future letters from the IRS asking for updated financial information, you must not ignore them.

Compliance

In all cases, and whatever repayment program you are accepted into, remember your obligations. You ignore IRS conditions at your peril! You ignore IRS letters at your risk!

If you don't stay in compliance with those programs, they could drop you from the program, and you revert to a tax-delinquent status. The full amount is again due.

Alternatively, the IRS might request additional information to see if you still qualify for the program. The IRS can request additional information periodically (every two years or so is common). What happens during those two years? You have to stay compliant in each current year, or you're delinquent again. Be careful with current-year filing extensions and respect the new deadline. If your extension requires you to file by October 15, don't miss it. If you are in an installment agreement and you are not in compliance, the IRS could send you a letter—one more dreaded letter! It will announce that you are not in compliance and that your installment agreement is in default.

If you're just floundering financially and can't stay compliant, the IRS will eventually start taking some type of collection action. If you are drowning in debt, you now know that you must proactively contact the IRS. Do it through a tax resolution specialist and grab that life jacket. The IRS will ask new questions, initiate a new process, and you won't know how to respond on your own.

At any time the taxpayer defaults on these resolution programs, the IRS will pick up where you left off at that new balance—unless you are in a reduced-tax-due program. In that case, you might find that you are back to owing the full amount. Interest and penalties accrue on the balance due, and over time, those amounts could put you right back where you started (or in a worse debt position).

I've added a chart below to give you an idea of how the programs might work for you.

IRS INSTALLMENT AGREEMENT (IA) OPTIONS

Plan Type	How Much You Owe	How Payments Work	Financial Info Required?	IRS Tax Lien Filed?
Simple Installment Agreement (SIA)	Up to $50,000	Monthly payments set by the IRS. Must be paid off before the collection deadline.	No	No (usually)
Non-Streamline Installment Agreement (NSIA)	Up to $250,000	Monthly payments over a longer period, still paid before the deadline.	No	Yes
Partial Payment Installment Agreement (PPIA)	Up to $250,000	Monthly payments based on what you can afford. Balance may not be fully paid.	Yes	Yes
Guaranteed Installment Agreement	Up to $10,000	Payments spread over up to 3 years. IRS must approve if you qualify.	No	No

Who Can Help with the IRS?

Only three types of professionals can officially represent a taxpayer to the IRS: a CPA, an Enrolled Agent, or a tax attorney.

You now know that I am an EA—an IRS-certified Enrolled Agent. This means I have federal authorization granted by the IRS to represent taxpayers before the IRS in all federal tax-related matters. That includes tax audits, appeals, and collections (tax-debt resolution processes).

EAs specialize in what the IRS calls "tax research" or tax laws. We are educated in tax laws by the IRS itself. Then we get tested on tax laws, and when we pass the tests, we are given the IRS's highest credential: Enrolled Agent.

How We Work with You

Before I start any work on tax resolution with clients, we sign an *IRS-recognized representation agreement*. The client agrees that I am their official representative to the IRS. I send the IRS the agreement, and all correspondence the IRS would normally address to the client henceforth comes to me until the case is resolved.

The first thing I do with clients is sit for a consultation with them. They've told me what their issue is—a past tax debt to settle, an audit to manage, etc. That first consultation is usually free. I explain the whole process of what I do and how I do it. I explain what I need them to do in the process. I talk about the cost of representing them (and no, I won't do so here; it is variable according to the needs of each case).

I have a disclaimer to make here about hiring an EA or other professional to resolve your tax debt. Here it is: *We can't work in a void.*

It's my job to help you keep your head above water, but you have to hold onto the flotation device too. When I represent you, it is all about communication and honesty.

It's your job, once you're in a debt-resolution program, to stick like glue to the terms. To sum it up, if you default on any of these programs:

1. The IRS drops you from the program.

2. You should immediately consult me to get back into the same or a different program.

3. IRS requests additional information every two years or so.

4. You have to stay in compliance with the current and future tax years (regardless of past tax due).

5. If you file for an extension, you must respect that new date.

6. Penalties and interest accrue, nonstop, until that back tax is paid in full.

Stated differently, I can help you get into a program. You are the one who stays in the program. I can give you a life jacket. You are the one who must wear it. I can help you get your head above water while you swim. It is your own swimming that gets you safely to shore.

You must *collaborate* with me to resolve your tax debt. There are things only I can do to move the process forward.

There are things only you can do to keep the process moving forward.

The Three-Step Process

After you hire me and we have a signed representation agreement, I have three different steps I take to help you get compliant.

Step 1

The first stage is my investigation or discovery. That's where I'm gathering information from you, the individual taxpayer, or you, the company owner. I also contact the IRS (which the representation agreement now allows me to do for you) to gather more information they have on file for you around this issue.

Step 2

The second stage is compliance verification. Sometimes people are not in compliance with the IRS and have a past-due tax debt. That's one reason clients need me. But sometimes, people are being audited, and I assist clients in navigating that audit process. Clients are sometimes surprised at being audited because they believe they're in compliance. I verify this. I want to know if you're filing and paying your personal income taxes on time, or if you're filing and paying your company payroll and other taxes as required. Compliance for audits generally refers to your standing for the last six years unless the IRS gives a different time frame.

Step 3

The third stage is the resolution step. We'll see how your issues can be resolved. We'll look at one or more programs you are potentially eligible for. We'll do the paperwork involved in applying for the program. I'll be there when the IRS requests any additional information to assess your eligibility.

I'll get you started by explaining your obligations in the program—and the risks of not sticking with it until full repayment is made.

Each case is somewhat different. I don't ever promise the client any particular program, outcome, or timeline for resolution. That's almost impossible to guarantee. There are many moving parts to a resolution, and I need to analyze the whole situation.

Say, for instance, a client receives a letter from the IRS. They're scared and also confused. They want me to interpret that letter. I can interpret it, but I still don't have the full context and I haven't done any research yet. In this kind of case, I tell people, "Let's just see what your situation is first. Let's sign a representation agreement so I can question the IRS on your behalf. While we're waiting for their response, bring me this list of documents and information from your records."

As your Enrolled Agent and tax resolution expert, I'm really a detective. As part of this third step, I'm also a money-management consultant who helps you straighten up your finances. You learn to use budgeting and other tools so that you don't fall into a tax-debt trap again in the future.

I can help you get into a program, but I can't keep you in the program. I can give you a life jacket to prevent you from drowning, but I can't force you to wear it. I can help you get your head above water while you swim, but it is your own swimming that gets you safely to shore.

CHAPTER 8

THE LETTERS THE IRS SENDS

Oh, those IRS letters! Are they scary? Yes. Are they scary only because you have a tax problem? No. As Elesha has demonstrated, they are *intentionally scary* in an effort to get you to take action, to communicate with the IRS.

This said, the IRS doesn't use frightening language only in its snail-mail paper letters to your home or business. It uses it online, too. One of my clients logged into her IRS portal and saw a bold notice across the top of her screen:

> *"Your Account is in Jeopardy of a Lien or Levy"*

It went on:

> *"Please pay immediately by bank account, by card, or set up a payment plan, if applicable. Resolve your balance, or*

we may file a notice of federal tax lien (if we have not already) and levy your assets."

Her heart dropped. Fear took over. Look at the screenshot below. What would your reaction have been to such a screen on *your* online tax portal?

She knew she was in arrears. "Now or never," she thought. Without hesitation, she grabbed the phone and rushed to contact the IRS to secure a payment plan.

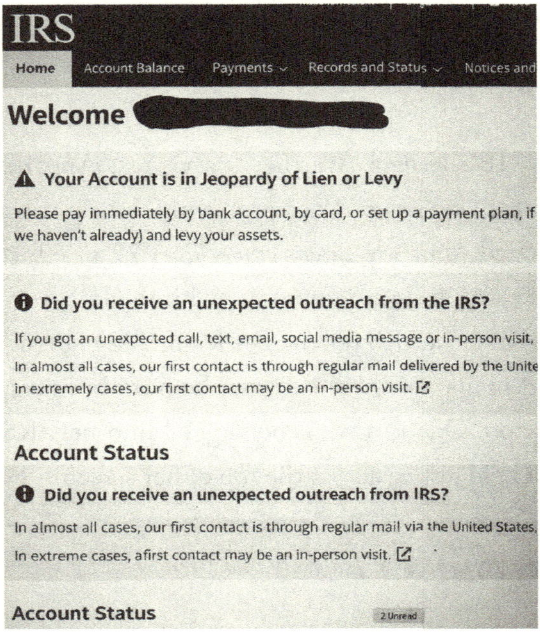

Elesha has taken you into the psychology of fear, but let me repeat this: The IRS uses language like this to *get you to take action.* It is in their snail-mail paper letters. It is in their digital, tax-portal messaging too.

The IRS is first and foremost a collection agency. If they don't collect your fair share of taxes on behalf of the government, they're not doing their job.

Letters from the IRS

That is language you might read online. Here are ten types of IRS letters that arrive in your mailbox.

CP14: The Balance Due reminder letter

I'm writing this in October. Earlier, I mentioned that I had just received twenty-five IRS letters for my clients. Those are the clients who should have filed in April, and they did. But they only sent a tax form. They never paid the amount the tax form stated was due. Those are **CP14** letters I'm getting now for their accounts. Penalties already apply with the arrival of this letter.

CP501: The second Balance Due reminder

Letter CP501 typically arrives between four and six weeks later, if you have not been in touch with the IRS. Increased penalties apply, and interest is accruing at this point. All the amounts are noted in that letter.

CP503: The third and final Balance Due reminder

Receiving this letter four to six weeks after the CP501 means you still haven't taken any action, with penalties increasing and interest still accruing.

CP504: Now it starts getting a little nasty

It is the final notice before the levy occurs. For an individual taxpayer, it's the payroll levy, the wage garnishment. For a business, it will be the bank account levy. It is also in letter CP504 where some things can happen due to the IRS being first in line for collections. They beat out every other creditor if you have a federal tax debt. The IRS is able to take your state tax refunds if you have a state income tax. If the state hasn't sent you your refund check yet, the IRS can seize it.

You see from these four letters that everything has a certain sequence. Ninety-nine times out of a hundred, the IRS will follow this sequential procedure of contact. If they continue to not hear from you or your representative (that would be me as your official representative), the sequential letters keep arriving. The penalty percentage rate keeps increasing. The interest keeps adding up.

With letter CP504, you have received a final notice before a levy. You also have a deadline to meet. However, if you ignore it—if you haven't contacted a tax resolution professional and hired them to take action—letter number five comes next.

CP90, LT11, or 1058: Notices of intent to levy; right to a hearing

The number on the letter depends on which department of the IRS sent it. So it could be with the automated collections department (CP90), or it could be with an actual revenue officer (LT11 or 1058).

These notices are important. The right to a hearing notification is a way for you to use your rights to say, "This is incorrect," but it is also a way to stop the IRS from taking any new action against you for a period of time. This is where the taxpayer can use their right to challenge the notice. It is where you ask for the levy actions to pause. The right to a hearing is valid as long as you respond to that letter within thirty days from the date on that letter. If, again, you ignore the letter and don't respond, you lose all the rights to any hearing when the thirty days expire.

If a client came to me in plenty of time, I would get the agreement to represent them signed and request a hearing on their behalf. I'd do this even before really studying their case or seeing their paperwork because that pause in IRS actions gives us time to study the client's circumstances.

A client came to me on day seven after receiving this particular letter number five, the "Intent to Levy; Right to a Hearing" letter.

He had sold his home for $740,000. This was not a taxable event in his state of residence nor at the federal level. He knew that, but his knowledge was incomplete. He was still required to report the amount and the source on his *federal* tax form. He did not because he was unaware that he was required to do so. Ah, the risks of doing your own taxes! Ignorance of the law, as they say, is no excuse for breaking the law.

The IRS looked at this as "underreported income." The whole $740,000 became taxable. Talk about a financial catastrophe! Now he owed the IRS $250,000. Any profit he may have imagined making from the sale of the home? Gone. And then some.

Since he was under audit for the $740,000, he could no longer file an amended return. That privilege was gone once the audit started (triggered by letter CP2000, which I discuss below). He had been trying for a couple of years to get the tax problem resolved. He was not successful. That's when he found and hired me. Once I had gathered all the documentation and completed all the required steps, we were still within the thirty-day response window.

Now, remember that this letter also tells you about your right to a hearing, a *Collection Due Process (CDP) Hearing*. I requested a CDP hearing for this client.[21] Having collected all the documentation that I needed for the hearing, I was able to get that case resolved. His house sale was no longer taxable. This was largely possible because he had the paperwork that we needed.

---

21 This references this letter's notification of their right to a Collection Due Process (CDP) hearing. This is an administrative hearing with the IRS Independent Office of Appeals, where a taxpayer can dispute a proposed tax levy or a filed federal tax lien. This is the taxpayer's opportunity to propose alternatives, such as a payment plan or an offer in compromise. It exists to make sure the IRS followed the law and to give the taxpayer a fair chance to be heard before enforced collection continues. FAQs appear here: https://www.irs.gov/appeals/collection-due-process-cdp-faqs. My process for requesting this hearing follows the rules stated here: https://www.taxpayeradvocate.irs.gov/notices/collection-due-process-cdp/. Accessed December 2025.

CP91: Announces the IRS's action of garnishment of your Social Security income

This letter's action works in combination with letter number five. Contrary to popular misconception (or hope), your Social Security income is not a protected income. If a person's only source of income is Social Security, the IRS is not allowed to garnish it. If the individual has other income, however, and that income isn't enough to satisfy the tax debt, the IRS can go after part or all of your Social Security. If, for instance, the delinquent taxpayer has an annual income of $100,000 and is also receiving Social Security, the IRS could possibly garnish that whole Social Security payment. This might be the case when the tax debt is much higher than the annual income. It just depends.

I have seen both cases—partial and full levy of Social Security—happen.

All the previous letters are about levying your financial assets so that the IRS tax debt is paid. The remaining letters I'll present deal with other types of situations. All of them are still about the IRS ensuring that they collect your back-due tax money.

Letter 3172: A notice of federal tax lien

We saw earlier that a lien is a way for the IRS to protect their interests. The IRS is first in line before all other collection agencies. But the IRS has legal ways of protecting its interests from other creditors you may have. One of them is to put a lien on property *equal to its resale value*. They know if you own a home or other real property. They don't want you to sell that real estate and run away with the cash when you still owe them tax money.

If you have property that's worth $200,000, the IRS will place a lien on the property that effectively blocks you from selling it behind their back. The IRS protects that asset because you might owe $300,000. The IRS wants to make sure that they get paid either before you sell that property or at the time you sell it. You have no authority to sell it without the IRS allowing it.

If the IRS has a lien on that $200,000 house, there's something called a *discharge*. You can get a "discharge to sell." That informs the buyer that you are authorized to sell. Or, if you're trying to refinance your home, it's called "a subordination." It basically tells the refinancing company that you have permission to refinance in spite of the federal tax lien.

The bottom line here: If you own property such as real estate and owe federal taxes, it doesn't matter how much the property is worth. As long as you don't pay the IRS, it will place and keep a lien on that property.

CP2000: A notice of underreported income

Let's say that when you filed your tax return, you missed something. You didn't report some income. I've mentioned this in previous chapters: In our digital world of many cross-references, *the IRS knows how much you should be declaring*. They know from one or more third-party filings that third-party So-and-So reported paying you X amount of income. If you didn't turn around and also report it to the IRS, they know.

Also, don't assume no one else reported it because it was "a small amount" or because "it was cash." A diligent business knows when it's paid a 1099 worker $600 or more and declares it. Don't assume that any type or amount of income can slide through undetected. It could be from an employer. It could be profits from stock or other investments. It could be from Social Security. Even if it was a cash payment (under the table), the IRS has ways of figuring out, tracking, calculating, and homing in on who paid what to whom and who didn't declare as required.

In letter CP2000, the IRS tells the individual or the business how much they should have reported according to the IRS research and cross-referencing.

If you don't correct or dispute the IRS numbers, you can expect an audit. If you have no documentation to prove your filing was correct, you can expect an audit. If you ignore their letter, you can expect an audit.

CP3219N: A notice of deficiency

Importantly, letter CP3219N is when you have another opportunity to defend your rights.[22] You have an option to petition the tax court.[23]

22 https://www.irs.gov/individuals/understanding-your-cp3219n-notice. Accessed December 2025.

23 https://www.taxpayeradvocate.irs.gov/notices/letter-3219/. Accessed December 2025.

I get excited at this point for my clients. This is what I call "*the secret sauce*." Why a secret sauce? The tax court is where cases are won and settled. Yet people are afraid to take this step. It is a common misconception that "going to tax court" is expensive. Tax court only costs $60! When I tell clients this, they are shocked. They also don't realize that the tax court is independent of the IRS.

Those delinquent taxpayers stop right there. But letter CP3219N is the secret sauce giving you ninety days to respond to the IRS. It is that letter that gives you the opportunity to take the IRS to tax court.

Many people, when they hear the words *tax court*, say, "I don't want to go to court. I don't want to pay those high fees. I don't want to pay an expensive attorney. No, sir! I don't want to have anything dealing with the IRS where I have to dispute this in any court of law. I don't want to deal with it." Yes, whoever says *tax court* thinks attorney. This is where it might seem a little scary for people. It is also where I can save you a fair bit of money in attorney fees.

I'm currently dealing with seven of my clients in this CP3219N stage of dealing with their tax debt. There is a tax court petition that the petitioner (you) must fill out correctly. Taxpayers don't know how to complete it. They don't know what the process is going to be. They don't know where to go. It is definitely not a DIY opportunity.

Important disclaimer: I'm not an attorney. I keep stressing to clients that I'm not an attorney. However, I can help them complete the petition that starts the tax court process. Taxpayers don't understand what information needs to go into the petition. I do.

Once the tax court has received your completed, signed petition, your case goes to tax court.

The tax court hearing resembles a trial, but for small cases ($50,000 or less is the rule of thumb, but the amount is at the court's discretion), procedures are streamlined and less formal.

It is basically a three-step procedure.

1. You (or your attorney/representative) present evidence and arguments about why you do not owe the tax as calculated by the IRS. You can bring documents, records, and witnesses.

2. Then, the IRS presents its side of the case and provides any supporting documentation for its proposed changes.

3. A judge makes a decision based on the evidence from both sides.

If you still don't believe the judge's findings are fair, you can appeal.

From the appeal, the case goes to settlement. "Settlement" is often misunderstood by taxpayers. It is not a required step, but an option during the appeals process. If one of my clients appeals, and both the client and the IRS agree to mediation, it takes place. This is when I'm able to step in as your representative to present the evidence.

Settlement = Mediation.

Two of those seven clients I mentioned are getting pretty close to settlement through mediation. However, even before the government shutdown, they had been in this process for a long time. I had five or six different appeals officers contact me, but the cases never got resolved. Those cases will be resolved during a mediation meeting. If no agreement is reached during mediation, it will go back to appeals. The judge will say, "Listen, people, we need to get this resolved," and then make sure a definitive resolution is reached.

The tax court process is an important asset for the taxpayers who can and wish to defend their interests.

668W: The garnishment announcement

Letter 668W is sent when the taxpayer has not taken appropriate action (i.e., has ignored previous letters). That was my case, and you know how well that went over with Elesha!

The employer will get this wage garnishment announcement via its own IRS letter. They'll be required by law to start garnishing your wages according to IRS stipulations. Garnishment could be continuous until your back taxes are paid in full or until you take other action to resolve your issue. As you know, I called the authorities, which effectively paused garnishment of Elesha's pay. It had come this far with my debts and my procrastination.

Now this garnishment is going to become a line item deduction on your payroll stub or payroll summary. Less money is deposited as wages in your account. You read how little remained of Elesha's paycheck after garnishment.

There is an equivalent for businesses, and the IRS looks at their payables and receivables. The difference between the wage garnishment and a business-type garnishment is that the individual employee will still get a portion of the paycheck. In business garnishment, the IRS will seize all funds it can locate until the tax debt is fully paid. For instance, if the business has invoiced some client or other party for $10,000 and has not yet been paid by them, the IRS will go to that party and say, "Pay us the ten grand." The IRS will not hesitate to take the whole amount and to repeat this with other accounts receivable until your business's tax bill is paid in full. Don't forget the legal ability of the IRS to empty your business bank account through a levy too.

There Is a Purpose

Each of these letters, all by itself, is scary. Each one maps out actions the IRS wants you to take. Each one has a purpose, and that is to use fear as a motivator for your action.

The bottom line is to stay compliant with your state and federal tax obligations. The IRS monitors individual taxpayers and businesses. You stay compliant with your tax obligations by fulfilling the following responsibilities:

1. Declare your whole income, whatever source(s) it came from.

2. File your paperwork on time (your 1040s or other required tax forms).

3. Pay your fair share of taxes, as calculated, and pay in full, on time.

4. If you have payment difficulties, communicate with the IRS *before* they contact you.

5. Year after year, stay current on your filing and payments.

6. If ever you get a letter from the IRS, open it and act on it right away!

Being in compliance with your federal and state tax obligations is fairly simple if you earn a salary. It's a bit more paperwork and filing for a business or for someone working as an independent contractor. In the end, it is all about having an intention to be and remain compliant. It's about understanding that help is available not only to file or correct a declaration but also to resolve back tax issues.

PART THREE

DR. ELESHA ROBERTS

Taking Proactive Steps to Beat the Fear

As Kevin learned and has shown you, taking steps to resolve a past tax issue or federal debt is *simple.*

But as I can acknowledge with you, it is not *easy.* You are fighting your emotions. You are fighting with your pride, which is telling you that you are smart and should be able to take care of this without any outside help. You are fighting your mind, which is making you bury your head in the sand.

Don't let your mind be the boss of you. You are smart. Take charge. You need to be the one who tells your mind what is going to happen.

This proactive step is called *changing your mindset.* Let me give you some guidance from both my professional and personal experiences to reset your thinking, so that you can take the actions that you must.

CHAPTER 9

CHANGING YOUR MINDSET

What is mindset? It's how you think about and view a situation, whether it's good or bad. When you're thinking about the IRS and letters sent by them, or just thinking about what a financial mess you've gotten yourself into, your mindset matters. Your mindset generally shifts to the negative, to what you cannot control.

I want to tell you that you can control your mindset. You can control how you think and what you think about. In fact, you are the only one who can control that.

Your thoughts may be jumbled. You may think to yourself, "This can't be right. How did this happen? The IRS won't really put me in jail or take my hard-earned money. I can't believe I put my family into this situation!" This may go on and on in your mind. Your mind is spinning and causing you to feel shame, guilt, anger, anxiety, and fear. You may also want to blame yourself or others for this situation. This negative mindset cannot solve your IRS problems.

Mindset: Tips and Tricks

Reframe

One of the things that I like to do when my mind is focused on a negative situation is to reframe my thought process.

Let me be the professor for a minute. In psychology, we talk a lot about *cognitive reframing,* also called *attributional retraining.* A study was performed with individuals dealing with the financial and emotional burden of student/college debt.[24] Researchers wanted to determine whether cognitive reframing techniques would improve the individuals' perceived wellness and mindset around academic challenges. That is a very brief and incomplete summary of the study, which you can review on your own if you are interested. However, the results of the study indicated that these mindset reframing techniques improved the participants' sense of academic control, academic hope, and overall course achievement. The techniques enhanced participants' cognition (thoughts/mindset), their affect (emotions/mood), and their performance outcomes.

This reframing process, in simple terms, involves taking a negative mindset and changing it into something

---

24 RP Dryden et al., "Assisting Students in Debt to Overcome Academic Setbacks With a Cognitive-Reframing Motivation Intervention," *Journal of Educational Psychology* 115, No. 1 (2023): 55–72, https://psycnet.apa.org/doiLanding?doi=10.1037%2Fedu0000770. Accessed December 2025.

more positive (reframing it). This takes practice. You must be intentional about reframing your thoughts to change your feelings and mindset about a situation. This will ultimately impact the actions that you decide to take. Don't let negative thoughts or feelings slide. You must deal with each thought as it comes. This requires you to make a conscious effort. You must tell yourself, "I don't want to think like this. This thought process will have negative consequences. I must be positive and deal with this issue head-on."

This may require you to shout out loud the word "Stop!" During this time, you may mentally and/or physically throw your hands up and shout "Stop!" Some people use rubber bands worn around their wrist as a physical cue to stop a negative thought process. In this situation, they pull and snap the rubber band to send a signal to their brain to reframe things.

Reframing is a way to give yourself a pep talk. This helps to stop self-sabotage and personal trash talk. Instead, I like to say things like, "You know you can do this. You can accomplish this. You can find help. You have done hard things before and succeeded."

Another reframing strategy that might work well for you is to keep a notebook or journal full of positive affirmations. You may want to open the notebook and read from it anytime you need to reframe a negative thought. Individuals who use this strategy might also repeat positive quotes or phrases like a mantra to themselves. This works well to reframe those negative thoughts, especially when your mind is beating you up, when you feel defeated, or when you want to give up.

My aunt, one of the strongest and most resilient people that I know, used a similar reframing strategy when raising her son (my cousin). My aunt's husband (my uncle) passed away at a very early time in their marriage. He was in a fatal motorcycle accident. During that time, her focus had to shift from herself to raising her son. He was young, and she figured she was going to have to raise him by herself. She was set on helping him to be the best man that he could be without having his father around. One thing that my aunt did was to write positive affirmations, biblical scriptures, and other messages on Post-it notes (small, colorful sticky notes), which she placed all around her house for her son to see. She would write positive phrases like, "You are somebody! God is good! Focus on the solution, not the problem. You are stronger than you know." She would put them on the walls of his room, the bathroom mirror, in the living room, kitchen, and near the front door. These notes helped to create (frame) positive self-esteem and a positive outlook on life for her son and others who happened to read the colorful notes. Growing up, we all thought this was funny; we often questioned the purpose of these notes. However, what she knew then was that a positive mindset makes a difference. She wanted to infuse as much positivity as she could into her son's mind to help him overcome negative, tragic, or life-altering situations that might arise. A negative or bad situation does not have to define you. My cousin, no longer a boy but a strong man, is full of confidence and resilience. I strongly believe these notes made a difference in shaping and transforming his mindset.

Break Avoidance

The next way to help you get out of debt and manage your finances is to think about methods that can be used to break the pattern of avoidance. You can control this pattern of behavior, since it, too, is all in the mind. Most of Kevin's clients (and Kevin himself during our debt crisis) had a mindset of avoidance. "If I don't acknowledge the problem, it really won't be a problem."

When my paycheck was garnished, that broke Kevin's procrastination. It broke his avoidance. It shattered his denial, as he had to come clean with me about the scope of our debt. He couldn't hide the debt anymore. First, we argued—which included some yelling—about the situation. Then we came up with a plan. We took action. In short, we turned the avoidance into action.

If you are in need of Kevin's services, that probably means you have already spent a fair amount of time in denial and avoidance of the debt problem. You no longer have the luxury to sit back and allow others to plan what you're going to do. Kevin will skillfully lay out the risks of not taking action for you.

You have to take an active role in what is going on with your finances. If you remain in denial too long, it's the IRS that will tell you what your plan is, and you won't like that one little bit! Asking for help is impossible when you are in denial and avoidance. Breaking the pattern of avoidance requires a change in your mindset.

Take Action

Taking action requires, again, a shift in your thinking, thought patterns, and behaviors. You have to make a mental decision. You must decide to take the steps needed to change your situation. Taking action tells your mind that you are in charge. You are the boss, and you are in control of the situation or issue.

Taking action and being proactive means you get in front of the problem. You come up with ways to solve it. However, if something is going on that you were not aware of, it can catch you off guard. I can attest to that. In my situation, I did not know that my family was drowning in debt. You may lose your bearings momentarily. You may react, as I did, with anger, negativity, and fear. It's human nature. Once you know you have a situation, you react with your emotions, then you get those out of the way so that you can take action. All your actions are focused on addressing the issue and solving the problem. You start to list the actions you can take now, tomorrow, and next week that move you toward solving the problem.

We have spoken about our plan earlier in the book. In our situation, this was a two-part plan.

Part One was the repayment plan Kevin agreed to with the Department of the Treasury for the SBA loan balance.

He was accepted into a repayment program. He signed off on the payment terms. Whatever you agree to with the IRS is what you commit to paying. You must stick with that IRS payment program until the debt is paid off. You must communicate with the IRS if your situation changes in a way that might affect your commitment.

Part Two was, for us, simultaneous with Part One. This involved paying off our personal credit card debt and his personal (non-SBA) bank loan. That was a substantial debt, as Kevin had maxed out his and my credit cards to finance his business. Having maxed out the cards and his ability to get personal loans, he turned to that SBA loan. However, our prior debt didn't go away on its own. During Part Two of our plan, we used the snowball approach to debt elimination.[25]

Here are the steps to snowballing yourself out of debt:

Step 1

List your debts from smallest to largest (regardless of interest rate). Credit cards plus Kevin's personal loan were our focus.

Step 2

Make minimum payments on all listed debts *except* the smallest debt.

---

25 We used Dave Ramsey's advice found in this blog on his website: "How the Debt Snowball Method Works," August 19, 2025, by George Kamel. https://www.ramseysolutions.com/debt/how-the-debt-snowball-method-works?srsltid=AfmBOopVnvNCQVdOFb7SOClMvF-fI0RmfZLh3kEpxFGTY1YEwUt5dKFVw. Accessed December 2025.

Step 3

Throw as much extra money as you can on your *smallest* debt until it's gone. NOTE: You must make a payment amount greater than the minimum to get ahead! When it is paid off, cross it off your list.

Step 4

Take what you were paying on your smallest debt and add that to your usual minimum payment on the next-smallest debt until it's gone too. Throw any "extra" money that you get at this debt. Cross it off and move to the next debt.

Step 5

Repeat until each debt is paid in full.

It was by using the snowball approach that we started to see light at the end of the tunnel early in year two of our plan.

To summarize the actions we took:

- We followed the Department of the Treasury program for Kevin's SBA loan repayment.

- We committed to our shared snowball plan to pay down credit card and personal bank loan debt.

- I worked three jobs to cover household bills and necessities.

- We jointly wrote and stuck with a cash-only budget.
- Kevin worked on building his business up.

Those were the actions we developed and started following right away. Was this challenging? Yes, but we kept moving forward. We were forced to take action every day, and that helped us build up a positive kind of momentum to tackle our debt. This was difficult, tiring, and often exhausting. But we did it.

Two Safe Places

Another mindset issue is thinking that you don't need help. We find ourselves saying, "I don't need debt-resolution assistance. This concern is not related to my mental health. I don't need mental health help because of my finances."

Is it okay to ask for help both with your IRS issue and your mental/emotional health? Yes. This might, however, require a shift in your thinking and mindset. You must make a decision to seek help.

For tax debt, you seek out a tax resolution specialist, which is Kevin's expertise. Talking to people who have lived with your same emotional and financial experiences is valuable. No secret about it now: Kevin has lived your experiences! Kevin's office is truly a safe place for his clients to lay it all out and create a plan of action.

I also think that talking to a mental health counselor is valuable. I'm a nurse. I understand that asking for this type of help may be challenging. Whether it is a counselor, a therapist, or a clinical psychologist, they provide a safe place where you can get clarity and put things in the right perspective. You can't solve a problem until you acknowledge it. You can't stick with a resolution plan if you are fearful or have constant negative self-talk. These professionals can help you work through each of these areas.

If you remain in denial too long, it's the IRS that will tell you what your plan is, and you won't like that one little bit!

Kevin and I discussed the need to seek professional help back then, while going through our debt issue. In the end, we did not do couples therapy. We chose to go to the same counselor, but separately. I think this really helped us early on, because we weren't at a point where we could be honest with each other about our feelings. Kevin had grief, shame, and deep anxiety related to our financial crisis. I had anger and fear. We worried about the other one's reactions. This was our first major crisis together. The counselor's office was our safe place to talk to someone else about what was going on. We worked through some of the feelings of being overwhelmed and vulnerable.

I believe that getting this expertise from a mental health counselor can be valuable for almost everyone. And for us, it was important to talk to somebody who had context, meaning that they knew what had happened with him, and they also knew our backstory. The counselor was able to use that information to inform how we thought about our situations individually and as a couple.

Communication: Tips and Tricks

You can't plan without discussion. Your very first step has to be those uncomfortable conversations. Take the emotion out of it. Stop the blaming game.

Kevin had to come clean with me and explain the mess he was in and how I was involved. You have to come clean with your spouse or business partner. You have to admit out loud, "I messed up. I got us into this debt. I was in denial about it. I consciously avoided taking action." Allowing time to go by without communicating with your spouse or business partner only makes the situation worse. You may choose to sit them down and say, "Okay. Here's what happened. Here's what I need you to know about the whole mess. Here's what you can expect. We now need to make a plan. We need a budget."

My position was, and still is today, that as a married couple, his problems are my problems and my problems are his problems. Learning how to talk about them as they come up means you've first burned through the emotional reactivity. You've let go of blaming, let go of denial, and stopped making excuses. You've reframed things.

We quickly understood that learning how to communicate and argue in the right way was important. I moved into an "adult" space where I could initiate a hard conversation. I'd be in the moment and very attentive when Kevin started the hard conversations. We both had to remove the emotions from our conversations in order to make a plan and work our plan.

We'd had that blow-up, and now it was about effective communication. That's why removing the emotional side of it is important. Now, with a cool head, you look at the facts of the situation.

After that garnished paycheck shock and my emotional outbursts, I approached my husband for the facts of this situation. I needed to know my role in moving us forward and out of debt. My head was (a bit) cooler, and we got into a calm discussion about our action plan.

Assemble Your Team

You must communicate about the debt and its resolution with the right people. I call it "assembling the team." You shouldn't navigate this difficult situation alone. You shouldn't leave others in the dark. That's why involving your business partner or spouse right away is important. With my garnishment, Kevin finally realized I was an involved party. I was a part of his team and therefore shared responsibility for resolving the problem.

Communication must be about how you approach the issue with a united front. You can have individual roles, but you really are targeting the problem together. There will be things that you need to work through with your spouse (or your business partner) as a team to accomplish the task.

Next, you need an expert to help you resolve the issue. Even when you consult an expert like Kevin, the expectation is that you will work closely with him to resolve your problem. He will do most of the heavy lifting to help you get organized and gather needed data to advocate for you. Your role is to discuss things openly with him and provide him with the information he needs. You will be involved with your resolution expert until your debt is gone.

Stay the Course: Tips and Tricks

Paying back big debt takes time, and you have to stay on the path. You can't keep all the details in your head. My most important tip is to write everything out.

Kevin is really big on spreadsheets. Oh, my goodness, he loves a good Excel spreadsheet! He listed everything we had to pay for on the spreadsheet, but my mind does not work in Excel. I love hands-on action, so actually seeing the notices and then asking Kevin to interpret them for me was helpful. His spreadsheet allowed us to know what to pay first and how much that was. That's how we managed the whole debt-snowballing process. I'd see the bill; Kevin would list it in Excel. He'd cross each one off as we paid it (not deleted! I wanted to see those cross-offs!). For me, there was something about physically touching the paper that clarified things. I liked seeing those items on a printout of his spreadsheet with a nice, thick cross-out line through them. It was gratifying to scratch it off the Excel list and put that bill or statement in a *PAID* file folder.

If you're like me—a big to-do list person—scratching those debts off that list is instant gratification. Kevin was highlighting that Excel tab in a different color. He was watching those debt totals go down, down, down while our available cash totals went up, up, up on his screen. That was the gratification for him.

The takeaway is that you must get really organized. Write it out. Everyone on your team (tax resolution expert, spouse, business partner) must be involved and *see* that progress is being made. It helps you stay on the path—stay the course.

Resiliency

To stay the course, you need stamina, emotional and mental focus, and a positive mind.

I know now from that experience with Kevin that emotional strength comes in more than one form. I thought I was a strong person. Then the garnishment and the cascade of debts that led to it came into my awareness. Facing and paying down that debt was our first big challenge as a married couple. We both took an emotional hit from it and felt vulnerable (confused, angry, scared . . . and a whole list of other emotions that we weren't used to).

We needed to be able to pivot and face this together. So calm-headed communication about every detail was the first key to staying strong and focused. That took mindfulness. I am really big on mindfulness. Mindfulness is paying attention and being in the moment. It's an alert state of awareness. You are 100 percent present in the moment. You are 100 percent attentive to talking with your spouse, especially when going into a challenging kind of conversation. You listen to understand. You question, not to insult or jab at your partner, but to get more information and understand fully.

Being present is being intentional about what you're going to talk about. You're intentional about what you're going to focus on in that time frame. You're going to do all of this in a calm state. Having a calm mindset is important. You might not work on every aspect of your plan or problem during one meeting. You're going to take pieces of it. You take one step at a time.

When I was in my PhD program, one of my advisors said, "The key to being successful in a doctorate program is looking at things one at a time." She had to tell us that. As adult learners, we were used to being multitaskers. She said, "I understand multitasking. But not here. Not to achieve a big, new, difficult goal." Paying down tax and other debts is a huge goal. Kevin and I had to focus on one thing at a time.

You need to be resilient for another vital reason: Debt resolution doesn't happen overnight. It took us years. It may take you just as long. You need to stick with the plan! Think of a bottle of glue, visualize it, and think about all the characteristics associated with that glue. Glue is sticky and often messy when it spills and gets everywhere. However, with proper help, it can be cleaned up, leaving very little residue. That's how we want you to think about your tax resolution program. If you can stick to the plan (created with and for you by an expert), stay intentional, and stay in that moment, then you will be successful.

That is what helped me stay resilient and keep going. It's what kept me talking with Kevin about our plan, our next goal, our next payment, our next crossed-off debt. It was remembering that glue analogy. This is how we attack all of our problems, even now.

Don't let this be like those fated New Year's resolutions, firm plans on January 1 and abandoned by February 1. You look at your debt-resolution plan on Day One and think, "Oh, yes, I can stick to the plan. By sticking to the plan, working my plan, whittling it down piece by piece, I will be successful. I will be able to do this." You also have to repeat these words and actions on *Day Two, Day Three, and all the days between*. This is what making a resolution is all about.

Stress Management

Stress management is related to resiliency. Stress management is all about using strategies to simplify overwhelming circumstances and unexpected events. The goal of effective stress management techniques is to stay calm and cool-headed—not to burn out, not to give up when faced with overwhelming odds.

Exercise and body movement are big tools for stress reduction. While going through our financial crisis, I decided to embrace physical activity and move more. While I did try to get outside more and walk, I achieved this largely by working more hours in a busy nursing unit. I was working so much. I was physically taking care of patients and doing tasks that required body mechanics and body movement. Looking back, I think that constant movement did help me. When I got home in the evening, I was physically exhausted. Kevin was exhausted too. We had no more energy to fuss or fight, which may have been a good thing.

I'm certainly not telling you to work to the point of exhaustion. I am also not saying to overexert yourself at work. However, there is something about staying busy and looking for things that can push you forward. Whether that's working at another job or doing a manual hobby that takes your mind off worries for a while, it does make a difference. We kept busy, we kept moving, and it was part of what made us successful.

After working so many hours, it is a great idea to treat yourself to a reward. Treating yourself from time to time can reduce stress. Think of all the ways you can treat yourself that cost very little or nothing. Think of calming activities that bring you joy, peace, and pleasure. After tackling one difficult task today, treat yourself to a walk through a beautiful park. Treat yourself by sitting with your child to watch a fun animated movie together. You may decide to treat yourself to a movie (without those expensive theater snacks!) and an inexpensive sit-down dinner. An occasional reward or treat like these are beneficial. The keyword is *occasional!* Try to reserve them for when you have accomplished a difficult debt-reduction task or when you have had a difficult conversation or a hard day. Conversations focused on budgeting and financial planning can be difficult. Rewarding yourself after these talks can be helpful to reduce tension and stress.

Having a spiritual foundation is also stress-reducing. Kevin and I believe in God. I believe that having some type of spiritual connection will strengthen every person. We have that spiritual connection; I do believe it has helped Kevin and me to be successful. Back then and today, we are always in church on Sunday, always in Bible study on Wednesday night. Despite working to excess back then, we still had our spiritual family. They may not have known everything that was going on. However, prayer, connection, and encouragement were always provided. This helped to break the tension in our relationship and decrease our stress.

Because of our faith, we knew that when everything was falling apart, we did not have to fall apart. We did not have to fall apart because we had a connection to God. This connection kept us grounded, centered, and trusting. We knew that God was always going to help us to figure out a way to provide for our family.

Whether that spirituality looks like prayer, church attendance, or reading a scripture at home every morning,

I believe in that power to support you. You can read many great Bible stories that talk about resiliency and overcoming challenges.

We knew that when everything was falling apart, we did not have to fall apart.

Goals

To get out of serious debt, you need a plan, and that plan needs to come with goals. Let's call them mini-goals that help get you to that one big goal of being in tax compliance and debt free.

Your first mini-goal should be to talk with an expert about your debt. You are drowning in debt. Get that buoy, that lifeline. An expert like Kevin is going to have a plan and a time frame for you. I know that for us, it was a long haul. Creating a plan and working on your goals will require patience, communication, resilience, a positive mindset, and the determination to stick to the plan.

Mini-goals and a step-by-step plan help when your big-goal time frame is long.

One constant on your list of mini-goals is staying on the path—staying the course, never giving up. If you want to give up, if your money situation changes for the worse during the plan, or if you're feeling overwhelmed in spite of it all, don't fall apart. Seek additional help from a mental health professional or from your tax resolution expert. Talk with your spouse or your business partner. Communication is key throughout the process to keep you on track. Take your stress-reduction steps. Set small goals.

Looking back, I equate the debt-resolution process to weightlifting to build muscle. That's something that I love to do. I love to work out. I love to lift heavy, heavy, heavy to build that muscle. If everyone could get those muscles overnight, they would. But it takes time, under pressure, to build that muscle. At every step, with every mini-goal you reach, with every crossed-out debt, your muscle gets stronger. You see that you are making progress, getting financially stronger. Be patient. Set and get mini-goals. Take the steps. Stay on the path. Do the work. Get stronger.

Trust is involved. First, trust yourself. Reframe that nasty self-talk into supportive thoughts. Turn willingly to a proven expert to guide you and then trust them to represent you to the IRS. Trust your spouse, your business partner, and your mental health professional. Respect them through your honesty. Protect your relationships. Respect your family. Be accountable for your actions.

Kevin and I are business partners. I am the business partner who doesn't want anything to do with his day-to-day business. My mindset is totally different from his. I have to trust in him. This means that I do not need to know everything about what he does. However, I still have to be aware of what is going on and how it will affect our family. I bring a different perspective and see things that he cannot see. I can be his sounding board. I add value to the business in a different way from an everyday partner. I know him, and we're always going to talk about everything after our major financial challenge. We talk about his business, my career, our life as a couple, and our family. It is a true partnership. It is a marriage where we share a lot of the same principles, the same beliefs, the same mindset.

Kevin and I have been married for twenty-one years, and we dated for five years before getting married. I know he's learned the hard lessons. I certainly have come a long way in how I view money and money management. We've both made huge strides in how we communicate with each other. Our bond is strong.

Have that as a goal you can reach: Beyond getting out of tax debt, you and your spouse or business partner should work as a team to face every challenge. Together, you can accomplish whatever goal you set for yourself, your family, your marriage, your career, or your business.

APPENDICES

Appendix I: A Summary of Common IRS Collection Notices

Appendix II: Steps to Take When Receiving a Collection Notice

Appendix III: Preventing IRS Collection Issues

APPENDIX I

A SUMMARY OF COMMON IRS COLLECTION NOTICES

I present each of these letters in Chapter 8 and here again in the Appendix. IRS collection notices are serious, so repetition never hurts. The action each letter asks of you is manageable with the right approach.

Understand what these notices mean and take proactive steps. This is how businesses can protect their business continuity. This is how individuals can protect their family's financial well-being.

If you are facing IRS collection issues, an IRS audit, or your first IRS letter in the mail, consult with a tax resolution expert to identify your options. Take immediate action to resolve the matter efficiently.

1. CP14: Balance Due Notice

What It Means

The IRS has identified that the client owes taxes, penalties, or interest and has not yet paid the full amount due. This is often the first notice in the collection process.

What Happens Next

- If the client pays in full or sets up a payment plan, the case is resolved.
- If ignored, additional notices (CP501, CP503) will follow, increasing penalties and interest.

2. CP501: Reminder of Balance Due

What It Means

A follow-up notice reminding the client that they still owe money. The tone is more urgent than CP14 but not yet threatening.

What Happens Next

- Continued inaction triggers the CP503 notice.
- Penalties and interest accumulate until the debt is addressed.

3. CP503: Second Reminder Notice

What It Means

The IRS has not received a response or payment after sending CP501. The notice warns the client that payment is required immediately to avoid further action.

What Happens Next

- Failure to respond leads to the CP504 notice, where enforcement actions (like liens or levies) are introduced.

4. CP504: Final Notice Before Levy

What It Means

A warning that enforced collection actions, such as levies or wage garnishments, are imminent unless the client responds within 30 days.

What Happens Next

- IRS has the ability to take state tax refunds.

- If no action is taken, the IRS can proceed with a final notice of intent to levy.

5. CP90/LT11/Letter 1058: Notice of Intent to Levy and Right to a Hearing

What It Means

The IRS formally notifies the client of its intent to levy assets (e.g., bank accounts or wages). Clients have 30 days to request a Collection Due Process (CDP) hearing.

What Happens Next

- If the client requests a hearing, levy actions are paused while the IRS considers alternatives.

- Without a response, levies of bank accounts or wages proceed after the deadline.

6. CP91: Final Notice of Intent to Levy on Social Security Benefits

What It Means

The IRS plans to garnish Social Security benefits to collect unpaid taxes.

What Happens Next

- Garnishment continues until the debt is paid or alternative arrangements are made.

7. Letter 3172: Notice of Federal Tax Lien

What It Means

The IRS has filed a tax lien against the client's property, granting a legal claim to assets until the debt is resolved.

What Happens Next

- Liens remain in place until the debt is fully paid or the IRS agrees to withdraw or subordinate the lien.

- Liens can complicate property sales or financing.

8. CP2000: Notice of Underreported Income

What It Means

The IRS has identified discrepancies between the income reported by the client and third-party sources, such as employers or financial institutions.

What Happens Next

- If the client accepts the adjustments, they must pay the additional taxes, penalties, and interest.

- Disputing the notice requires prompt documentation and response to avoid further penalties.

- If ignored, IRS will send CP3219N – Notice of Deficiency.

9. CP3219N: Notice of Deficiency

What It Means

The IRS notifies the taxpayer of the proposed tax liability from audit changes.

What Happens Next

- The taxpayer has 90 days to petition the tax court on unagreed items.

- If agreed or ignored, after 90 days, the IRS will assess tax.

10. Letter 668-W: Wage Garnishment Notice

What It Means

The IRS notifies the client's employer to begin garnishing wages until the debt is paid.

What Happens Next

- Wage garnishment continues until the balance is paid in full or a resolution is negotiated with the IRS.

APPENDIX II

STEPS TO TAKE WHEN RECEIVING A COLLECTION NOTICE

1. Do not ignore it. IRS notices will not go away on their own. Ignoring them leads to additional penalties and enforcement actions.

2. Verify the information. Compare the notice with your tax records to confirm the accuracy of the amount due.

3. Consider your payment options. These include full payment, an installment agreement, or an offer in compromise.

4. Seek professional help. A tax professional can help negotiate favorable terms and protect your assets.

5. Respond promptly. Meeting deadlines is crucial to maintaining your appeal rights and avoiding enforcement actions.

APPENDIX III

PREVENTING IRS COLLECTION ISSUES

- Stay current with tax filings. Ensure all required tax returns are filed on time.

- Pay estimated taxes. Business owners and independent contractors often have variable income; making estimated tax payments and paying them on time reduces the risk of unexpected tax bills.

- Keep accurate written financial records. Maintain thorough financial records to support deductions and credits.

- Address tax notices when they arrive. The sooner you act, the more resolution options you have available.

Get in touch with Kevin Roberts for a free consultation.

830-743-9993

https://mytaxlifeline.com/contact/

ABOUT THE AUTHORS

Kevin Roberts

Kevin Roberts is an Enrolled Agent (EA), licensed by the IRS, with over twenty years of experience in the tax industry. He specializes in helping to resolve individual and business state and federal tax problems and issues.

Over the span of his career, he has been a financial advisor, tax strategist, and budget analyst. In 2006, Kevin was a franchise owner and operator with multiple locations for one of the top tax preparation franchises. In 2013, he sold his locations to focus on representing taxpayers before the IRS.

His education and background have helped to prepare him for his role in the industry. Kevin received an MBA from Webster University in St. Louis, Missouri, and a BS (bachelor of science) from Wayland Baptist University in San Antonio,

Texas. Kevin also has his certificate as a Certified Tax Representation Consultant, or CTRC (signifying extensive training in the field of tax resolution).

Kevin served for nineteen years in two branches of the military, the US Army and the US Air Force.

Find more about Kevin and the tax relief lifeline he offers you at *https://mytaxlifeline.com/tax-resolution-firm/*. He won't let you drown in tax debt!

Dr. Elesha Roberts

Dr. Elesha Roberts is driven by a deep commitment to mental wellness and the belief that understanding stress psychology is the key to thriving in high-pressure environments. With a career spanning over two decades, she has dedicated herself to helping students and professionals master adaptive coping strategies to combat burnout and incivility.

Currently a clinical assistant professor at the University of Texas in the Austin School of Nursing and a former faculty member at Baylor University in Waco, Texas, Dr. Roberts blends clinical expertise with a passion for teaching.

She holds a PhD and a DNP, along with triple national certifications in nursing education and simulation (CNE, CNEcl, CHSE).

Dr. Roberts believes education should be dynamic and human-centered. She specializes in using simulation-based learning and creative visual arts to bridge the gap between theory and real-world emotion. Her work empowers individuals to improve therapeutic communication, build resilience, and navigate the complexities of mental health with confidence and cultural humility.

Elesha and Kevin have two sons, aged ten and fourteen. The whole family loves the water, doing lots of river rafting and swimming. Jackson (the older child) is an avid swimmer and captain of his high school swim team. Avery (the younger child) also swims competitively with a local swim team and enjoys basketball and computer gaming in his free time.

Made in the USA
Coppell, TX
13 June 2026

81314606R10100